THE
WEALTH
BLUEPRINT

*Everything you'll need to take control
of your portfolio and beat the
"Wall Street Pros" at their own game*

SELWYN GERBER, CPA

THE WEALTH BLUEPRINT

ISBN 978-0-615-47258-4

Invest right. Then sleep tight.®
is a registered trademark of RVW Investing LLC

Code: 1880+LNN:AIND

*This book is dedicated to
all the financial planners,
stockbrokers, and wealth advisors
I have met over many decades
who, unknowingly, showed me the light.*

*It is designed to be read or skimmed.
The highlighted boxes will provide all you need to know
in executive briefing format,
especially in the Executive Summary and Chapter 15.*

Special thanks to Cheston Mizel.

CONTENTS

Is the Market Overvalued?

Stocks have rocketed from their 2009 lows. Now two prominent market thinkers see two vastly different scenarios playing out. Who is right?

HIT THE BRAKES: Robert Shiller the Yale University Economist says stocks are expensive.

GO FOR IT: David Bianco of Bank of America Merrill Lynch says stocks are a bargain.

E.S. Browning
The Wall Street Journal, April 2011

The Pillars of RVW Investing

1. *Equity markets work.* In the long run, owning pieces of successful businesses has produced more wealth than almost any other passive investment.

2. *Indexing is the most efficient and effective manner to access those gains.* Stock-picking and market-timing don't work. Indexing is low-cost, tax-efficient, and diversified.

3. *Asset allocation is the most critical determinant of portfolio performance.* Selecting indexes covering a diversity of sectors and asset classes and providing global exposure works best. Enhanced indexing utilizes traditional capitalization-weighted indexes and other more complex indexes where components are included based on a true relative economic footprint. Bonds should be used to mute portfolio volatility and for target-date near-term withdrawal needs.

4. *Periodic rebalancing.* Restricting targeted properties of the various asset classes ensures that it is you who determines your relative asset allocation, rather than market movements.

5. *Be disciplined.* Adhere to your plan and ignore the headlines.

Preface

When I immigrated to the United States in 1977, the Dow Jones Industrial Average stood at about 850 points. Since then, it has risen in value some fifteenfold. By also reinvesting dividends you could have increased your investment more than twentyfold.

Over this period of time, the market has suffered several of the largest single-day point and percentage declines, weathered the chaos that attended the 9/11 attacks (which, unexpectedly, shut down Wall Street for the longest continuous period in history since the death of Franklin D. Roosevelt in 1945), and endured several significant domestic and international financial crises. Yet, in time, each of those downturns proved to be simply a compressed spring which propelled the market to reach new highs.

Sadly, most equity investors did not reap the benefits of those market rebounds simply because the ride that preceded them had been too turbulent, too gut-wrenching. They typically sold out . . . *at exactly the wrong times* . . . while others were poised to take full advantage of these buying opportunities and did just that.

Until six or seven years ago, my partners and I dutifully referred clients of our CPA firm to the leading stockbrokers and wealth managers, believing that they possessed superior tools and information to what we had. The results were almost always disappointing. We found an inverse correlation between the slickness of the marketing materials and the performance. "The penny dropped," and *RVW Investing* was born.

Profiting from Market Uncertainty

If the stock market has more than two consecutive losing days, you can expect the financial pundits and TV news anchors to begin their usual discourse on whatever crisis is at hand at the moment and complain how "the market hates uncertainty."

Such dialogue is ridiculous on its face. Although it is human nature to prefer a certain outcome over uncertainty, it is unrealistic to ever expect that there will be any certainty in the stock market. By this, I mean true certainty, such as summer follows spring, rather than the speculative certainty known as *conventional wisdom, group think,* or *mass hysteria.* The law of gravity demands that when you let go of something, it must fall to the ground. Any attempt to similarly constrain the stock market is illusory at best, and a snare for the unwary at worst.

In the 1720s, the South Sea Company's "right to all trade in the South Seas" was the next "sure thing," only to collapse entirely, leading the government of Britain to outlaw the sale of capital stock for more than a hundred years. On the cusp of the twenty-first century, the common belief was that any company (and its stock) connected to the Internet–the so-called "dot.com" boom–was on a rapid trajectory to the stars. As recently as 2006, to suggest that money might be lost by investing in real estate one risked being labeled an apostate. In the 1980s, the Japanese were believed to be on track to become the dominant world economy. All of this is the "certainty" that abides in an unrestrained economy.

THOUGHT FOR THE DAY

Stocks ought to produce higher returns than bonds in order for the capital markets to "work." Otherwise, stockholders would not be paid for the additional risk they take for being lower down the capital structure. It comes as no surprise, therefore, that stockholders have enjoyed outsized returns for their efforts.

– Rob Arnott, Investment Manager

In reality, uncertainty is just a substitute word for risk, and risk itself is highly correlated to reward, or at least the potential of reward. Without risk, there can be no reward. For this very reason, US Treasury bills–the shortest duration government debt–are described in economics textbooks as a "riskless" investment. When adjusted for inflation, their current expected return is zero or, even worse, negative. In periods of high inflation, the negatives could be extreme.

Uncertainty is the prize. In exchange for uncertainty, the investor understands that certainty offers little or no opportunity for gain. Indeed, without the speculative nature of risk, there would be no market. Imagine the nightmare of an "efficient-market hypothesis" in which there was no loss or no gain. What's the point of being invested if stock prices never change?

Conversely, to completely ignore the uncertainty of the market is folly. Investors must occasionally be reminded that the future is a mystery. Stock market "corrections," often influenced by external factors such as natural or financial disasters, are those reminders. Failure to remember the lessons of the past runs the risk of being swept up by the currently popular "hot" investment opportunity and its illusion of certainty, only to venture too close to the sun and melt one's wings . . . and come crashing back to Earth.

> Most investors think the risk is greater when the Dow is at 14,000 than when it is at 7,000.

The RVW Investor, in contrast to those looking for the next rocket to the stars, adopts a more realistic approach by accepting the uncertainty of the market and patiently awaiting its bountiful rewards, focusing instead on reducing risk through asset allocation, diversification, and "intelligent-indexing." After all, the best strategy is to invest with an appreciation for the way the market is, not the way we would like it to be. And that's just what we do at RVW Investing and what you will discover in this book.

The Secret of Investing in the Stock Market Summed Up in One Hundred Words

Figure 1-1 (p. 21) charts the history of the US stock market from 1926 through 2010. In that time, $1 invested in both large- and small-company stocks grew to more than $10,000. This represents stunning appreciation of almost 11% annually. But it wasn't always smooth sailing–there were severe headwinds along the way. And therein lies one of the keys to success: *always invest for the long term.* In fact, if you divide the market into ten-year periods, the market has posted positive returns more than 80% of the time–and there is no fifteen-year period in which it didn't appreciate!

> Even a stuck clock is right twice daily. The doom-and-gloomers have their moments of vindication every now and again. But then sanity and reason return and markets resume their long term upward march.
>
> – Rip Van Winkle Wisdom

The Seven Immutable Laws of Investing

1. *Beware of the Black Swan.* One-in-a-million random catastrophic economic events have been occurring very frequently over the past decade. The risk you take should never exceed your financial ability and psychological willingness to remain steadfast. The focus should not only be on the likelihood of an event happening–but of the consequences if it does.

2. *Transparency.* Never make any investment unless you fully understand it and all the risks it is exposed to.

3. *What the Big Print Giveth, the Small Print Taketh Away.* The more complex the investment, the faster you should fire the salesman. Complex products are designed to be sold, not bought. Complexity is designed to favor the issuer, not the investor.

4. *Risk Management.* Risk and return are not always related; it is risk and *expected* return that are related. Your portfolio should combine several uncorrelated risks and be fully diversified to minimize overall risk. Least-expected events are the ones that can really destroy plans–but in combination with other low-probability, independent risks they work powerfully to insulate from overall risk. Do not treat the highly improbable as impossible, nor the highly likely as certain.

5. *Discipline.* A well-thought-out strategy is always needed for successful investing, combined with the discipline to stay the course. The key is to resist the impulse to respond to the headlines by following the crowds who will go through successive bouts of greed and fear.

6. *Risk vs. Volatility.* Risk involves the permanent loss of principal, while volatility is a reflection of the crowd psychology that periodically underprices and then overprices your investments. Bear markets are a way of shaking out the weak investors and preparing the launching pad for the next bull run. Remember that history is on the side of the bulls over the long term. Investors assume that if their horizon were long enough, there is little to no risk. The result is that they take too much risk. Remember, just because something has not happened doesn't mean it cannot or will not. Individual stocks are risky no matter the horizon. *Indexes on the other hand have volatility but no risk–because indexes always eventually rise again.*

7. *Expenses and Taxes.* Although they may be minimized, expenses and taxes cannot be eliminated, and both affect return on investment. Reducing expenses increases returns. Longer holding periods and less activity result in lower capital gains taxes, maximizing profits.

Executive Summary

Everything You Needed to Know About Investing, But Were Working Too Hard at It to Ask

Indexing is an investment practice that aims to match the returns of a specified market benchmark. An indexing manager attempts to replicate the target index by holding a portfolio of the stocks in the index in the proportion owned by the index. This is often described as passive, emphasizing that the portfolio has broad diversification, low trading activity, and low costs.

Indexing as an investment practice has won acceptability in the last three decades as the mechanical outgrowth of the body of academic insights about markets and managers. Indeed, it was one of the first ideas to be propounded by finance academics from their empirical studies. They pointed out that the average manager would produce below-average results due to expenses, and above average managers would be identified and given more assets until they, too, became less than average.

For most stock investors, the Dow Jones Industrial Average returns for the past decade have left them feeling about the same as they did following their first root canal. It was a wild, roller coaster ride of ups and downs, ending not much higher than it began.

On January 14, 2000, the news media were in a frenzy, reporting that the Dow closed at an "all-time high" of 11,723 and, following one of the most turbulent periods of volatility, went on to reach its true record high of 14,164 on October 9, 2007. After the subprime lending debacle and near-collapse of large portions of the financial services industry, the Dow hit its nadir in the past decade, falling to 6,547 on March 9, 2009–a spectacular drop of 54%–effectively erasing nearly all gains made since the late 1990s.

Today, once again, the venerable Dow stands below its all-time peak (and is about where it was in 1999). Functioning in stealth mode, however, the S&P MidCap 600® index is close to its all-time high reached in July 2007, and the S&P SmallCap 600® appreciated an astounding 77% over the past decade. In long-term studies conducted by market-watcher Ibbotson Associates, large stocks tended lying on the beach, playing golf, or even sipping whiskey at the local pub. Typically, a minor course-correction on an annual basis is all that's required. For a select few, investing is a love pursued with passionate devotion; for the rest of us, however, we might prefer to devote our time to family, hobbies, and recreation.

Nevertheless, most of us would consider the prospect of ignoring our portfolios to be irresponsible and a surefire recipe for financial ruin. Consequently, we either spend countless hours wrestling with our investment decisions or we put our faith in the hands of "professional money managers," usually with disappointing results.

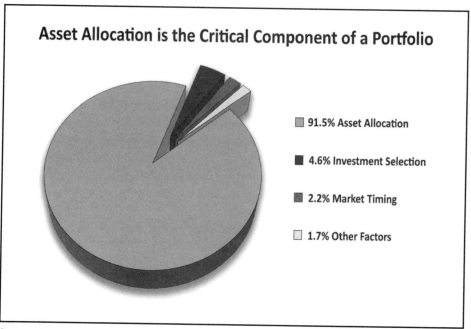

Source: Financial Analysts Journal, May/June 1991

This graph stresses that asset allocation is the most significant factor in determining portfolio returns rather than stock selection or market timing.

What if there were a way to structure your finances with clarity and confidence, knowing that you would be better off twenty years from now . . . *by doing virtually nothing?*

Many of us were brought up to believe that success is a function of hard work. We have been taught that laziness is a deadly sin which promises to impede any progress in life. In fact, Washington Irving's famous character, *Rip Van Winkle,* is depicted as a floundering fool who falls into a drunken slumber for twenty years and awakens to discover a world that has moved ahead without him, while at the same time it barely noticed that he was even gone.

Rip Van Winkle is the anti-hero who teaches us that a life of inaction is a life wasted. Following his example will certainly not produce a life of astounding productivity, personal growth, or satisfying relationships. Yet, when it comes to investing, old Rip just might have something to teach us after all.

Financial markets behave in a manner that is often mystifying, both to the uninitiated and to the veteran alike. Most investors subscribe to the belief that through diligent research and analysis they can select the right stocks and the right managers, and even determine the right timing to make their investment decisions.

> Micro-managing your portfolio is akin to watching the second hand on a clock. Strategic asset allocation means looking at the hour hand.
> – Rip Van Winkle Wisdom

Empirical data prove this belief a fallacy. Nobel Prize-winning economists teach us that an investor's asset allocation has the most impact on portfolio performance. Stock-picking and market-timing have no real impact. In fact, over any ten-year period, an estimated 80% of mutual fund managers fail to beat their benchmark indexes.

Benjamin Graham is considered by many to be "the father of value investing" and the inspirational guide of Warren Buffett. He used an iconic investor, whom he called *Mr. Market*, to demonstrate the fact that a wise investor chooses investments on their fundamental value rather than on the opinions of others or the direction of the markets.

> Stock prices in the short run are a reflection of successive bouts of greed and fear of the marketplace.
> – Rip Van Winkle Wisdom

Graham constructed a parable which goes something like this: Think of yourself as the owner of a share in a business, in partnership with others. One of your partners, Mr. Market, might be described as a bipolar neurotic who, on any given day, will make an offer to sell you his share or buy yours. His moods fluctuate anywhere between the depths of depression and unbelievable optimism and ebullience. One day he will offer you a ridiculously high price to buy or sell, and the next day he might lower that price dramatically.

Graham's and Buffett's belief is that Mr. Market's judgment is clouded more by the mass psychosis of crowds or his own mood swings than by rational thought . . . and the wise investor is presented with incredible buying and selling opportunities.

In the short term, there is no question that selected strategies and certain managers can and will provide returns above the market as a whole. However, the cold, hard facts demonstrate clearly that over time, active strategies consistently fall short of their own market index benchmarks. Latter-day experts tend to agree that by simply owning index funds, patiently weathering the volatile tides of market activity, investors will assure themselves market returns that surpass those achieved by at least 80% of all other investors.

> Passive investing is a misnomer. Index investors eschew market-timing and stock-picking not out of laziness or passivity, but because those activities usually reduce returns and increase risks. A better name for it would be "Intelligent Investing."
> – David M. Blitzer, Chairman
> Standard & Poor Index Committee

This book seeks to debunk classical myths about investing by showing how and why active fund or portfolio management is a losing game. On the other hand, smart index investing, combined with patience and the willingness to ignore day-to-day fluctuations in stock prices, is a surefire strategy for long-term success.

This book is also intended as a beacon for those who find themselves befuddled with the financial uncertainty of modern times. It endeavors to replace the gobbledygook of the financial pages with a simple, straigh tforward recipe for successful investing which has withstood the test of time. The process we call *"RVW Investing"* is not about getting rich quickly–any such strategy can just as easily make one poor more quickly. *RVW Investing* is about investing for the long term–with discipline, logic, and peace of mind.

If you are already yawning and ready for bed, you might learn all you need to know by understanding the following six principles.

RVW Principle 1: *Markets Work*

Most investors spend countless, frustrating hours, and often rack up big losses, trying to predict and understand exactly how markets work.

They attempt to buy and sell the right securities at the right time. While a select few develop great skill at riding the waves, so to speak, most get battered about and remain mystified by the market's "secrets." Then they look to so-called gurus and experts to tell them where to invest, usually to no avail.

The radical truth I am here to convey is that *investing success does not require that you understand how markets work*. All you need to know is *that markets work*. Markets emerge from the economic activity of all their participants. Buyers and sellers determine for themselves the price at which they are willing to transact. Prices will always move according to the expectations of supply and demand. Sometimes their expectations are based on rational and objective criteria, while at other times the emotions of greed or fear may take hold.

What is critical to understand is that, in the short term, markets will either under- or overestimate the value of any particular security. This occurs as the result of imperfect information about the true value of a security at any given time or because conditions exist that spur emotional (perhaps irrational) decisions. Over the long term, however, markets will reflect the true value of the underlying securities as information becomes known and the swings caused by transitory emotions cancel each other out.

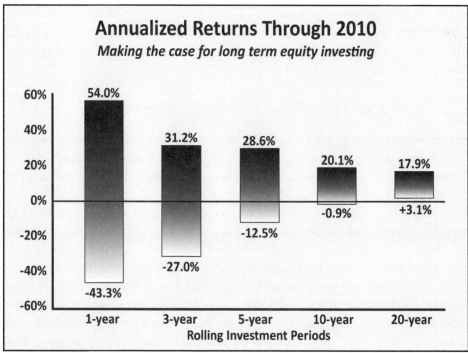

Source: RVW Research

A stock's price is theoretically a percentage of the underlying value of the company it represents. There are a large number of fundamental metrics–such as price-to-earnings ratio (P/E), growth rate, and price-to-sales ratio–that are used to evaluate the stock and attempt to ascertain proper pricing at any given time. Since market conditions and expectations of the future color the market's pricing of an asset, these fundamental metrics offer hardly any real objective value.

According to the University of Chicago's Center for Research in Security Prices (CRSP), from 1926–2010, slightly less than three years in every four (62 of 84) has shown a gain in the US stock markets, and there has never been a fifteen-year period in the combined history of the NYSE, AMEX, and NASDAQ with negative total returns.

CHANCE OF NEGATIVE RETURNS	
1-YEAR HOLDING PERIOD	26%
5-YEAR HOLDING PERIOD	14%
15-YEAR HOLDING PERIOD	0%

Source: CRSP

The most important thing to know is that as a company increases its earnings, the true value of the company increases. By extension, when the economy grows, the total value of the market increases. Once you understand that, over the long run, an investment in the market is an investment in the overall growth of the economy, you will begin to see the forest for the trees.

RVW Principle 2: *Stock-Picking Doesn't Work*

> Most investors pick last year's best managers and funds. That's like driving a car while looking in the rear-view mirror. Because of style rotation, it's a sure recipe for disaster.
> — Rip Van Winkle Wisdom

Conventional wisdom suggests that smart people generate good stock picks. Therefore, the more research a person does, the better his investing results will be. Likewise, a person expects that the best returns will come from hiring the best managers to do the hard work for her. It is true that there are some extremely talented individuals who have done quite well at the stock-picking game. That being said, the data are clear for the vast majority of those attempting to play: *stock-picking is a loser's game.*

For many years, *The Wall Street Journal* ran a "Dartboard Portfolio" in which the stocks were randomly selected by throwing darts at the stock listings. Those random portfolios regularly outperformed the educated picks of the "experts" and the stocks selected by the *Journal*'s readers.

Literally hundreds of studies have been conducted comparing active managers' performance over a ten-year period against the market's performance over the same interval. Time and time again, the market beat the managers. In fact, the odds of a particular manager beating the market over the long run are between 2.4% and 2.7%. By contrast, the odds of winning by picking any single number in roulette are 2.6%.

Few people would go to Las Vegas and bet their life savings on a single spin of the roulette wheel. So why bet on a manager who has the same chances of beating the market when you could just as easily choose an investment that will, at the very least, match the market?

RVW Principle 3: *Market Timing Doesn't Work*

The infamous adage in investing is: *buy low, sell high.* It is obvious to most that doing so is far easier said than done. Nevertheless, there are many who believe that it is possible to determine the optimal time to buy and to sell. Market timing, as it is called, is another art that many claim to have mastered but from which few have actually benefitted. In fact, there are hundreds of newsletters written by self-styled market-timing gurus who promise to inform readers of the exact moments of buy-sell opportunities. It is hard to ignore the fact that, if true, the predictions written in such letters would generate enough profits to dissuade those same gurus from exerting the effort to write them. Savvy investors view these letters with a great measure of skepticism.

The infamous adage in investing is: *buy low, sell high*. It is obvious to most that doing so is far easier said than done. Nevertheless, there are many who believe that it is possible to determine the optimal time to buy and to sell. Market timing, as it is called, is another art that many claim to have mastered but from which few have actually benefitted. In fact, there are hundreds of newsletters written by self-styled market-timing gurus who promise to inform readers of the exact moments of buy-sell opportunities. It is hard to ignore the fact that, if true, the predictions written in such letters would generate enough profits to dissuade the so-called gurus from exerting the efforts to write them. Savvy investors view these letters with a great measure of skepticism.

The data show conclusively that, over the short-term, markets move randomly, and when the equity markets move up, they tend to do so in significant spurts rather than in straight lines. Missing the thirty best trading days over a ten-year period ending in 2003 would have changed a significant gain of 160% for those who held on throughout into a loss of 8%.

> In the short term, the price of stocks has nothing to do with anything but the supply and demand of the available shares—which in turn are driven by alternating market cycles of euphoria and despondency. Sooner or later however, a company's true value will be indicative of its long-term earnings expectation and be reflected in its stock price.
>
> – Rip Van Winkle Wisdom

According to a University of Utah/Duke University study, 95% of market-timing newsletters did not survive beyond an average four-year lifespan. Moreover, Mark Hulbert, an independent newsletter tracker, followed the average returns of the picks from twenty-five newsletters that survived from 1988 through 1997, and discovered, not surprisingly, the newsletters delivered an average return of 11.1% versus the S&P 500®'s return of 18.1% over the same period.

There is no question that these letters are alluring, especially when they tout unbelievable past results. However, statistics don't lie. Attempting to time the market might be an entertaining pastime, but it is no way to invest the bulk of your hard-earned capital.

Additional recent academic research has identified measurable losses resulting from frequent trading. Using survey data involving a large sample of online brokerage clients, Arvid Hoffmann, Hersh Shefrin, and Joost Pennings determined that nearly all equity trading strategies manage to produce lower returns than the markets. Trading based on charting was the worst strategy. The raw net results of using trends and other chart patterns to predict returns was negative 0.92% *per month*. Trading based on financial news, intuition, or *professional advice* was the second worst, with a raw net return of negative 0.65% per month.

RVW Principle 4: *Long-Term Index Investing Provides Superior Results*

Most people think that selecting the right investments, watching them closely, and being prepared to reposition when necessary is the best formula for success. Without question, for those gifted with a healthy dose of prescience, this strategy will work quite well. Unfortunately, for the rest of us it is far removed from a foolproof endeavor.

The first mistake typical of most investors is their initial investment decision. When selecting a mutual fund, for example, people tend to look at those funds with the greatest (short-term) track record. Likewise, people tend to select stocks that have been recent top performers. The problem with this approach is that yesterday's top performers are rarely tomorrow's. Statistically, this is a big mistake, because hot sectors and portfolio strategies will go in and out of fashion with time. In fact, because of what is technically known as *style rotation* and *reversion to the mean*, the sectors that were hottest in the recent past tend to be the worst performers during the next market cycle of ups and downs.

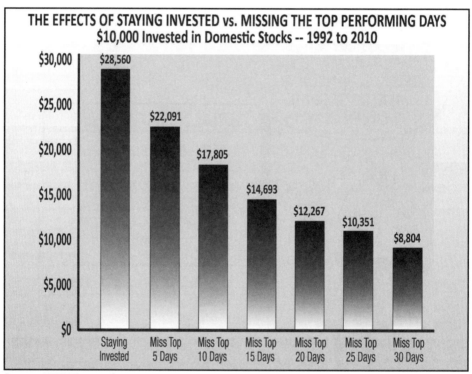

Source: RVW Research

The second common mistake active investors make is their failure to account for trading fees and taxes. As far as individual stocks go, sales commissions have become far more affordable with the proliferation of discount and online brokers. Mutual funds, on the other hand, are among the worst offenders at siphoning investor capital. Some mutual funds charge an upfront fee, called a *sales load*, that can be as high as 4%–8% of invested capital. Thus, moving out of funds in one mutual fund "family" into those of another fund family can be prohibitively expensive. Moreover, mutual funds also pay advisory fees internally to cover the expenses incurred in the management of the fund. These fees, averaging about 1% of annual net assets, result in "expense ratios" that can be as much as 0.5%–3% annually or more, and are often not clearly disclosed.

Even if transaction fees are minimized, taxes are another enormous drain. Whenever a security is sold, a tax liability (or loss) is incurred on the difference between the sales price and the initial purchase price (plus reinvested dividends and capital gains distributions, if any). When a security is held for more than a year it is taxed at the more favorable long term capital gains rate, which is significantly lower than the investor's marginal tax rate (the same tax rate generally applied to interest income and periodic dividends paid to investors). Tax liabilities erode long-term returns. Many active managers turn over their entire portfolios every year or two, assuring that any resulting net gains are taxed, most frequently, at their investors' highest ordinary income tax rates.

> There are three classes of people who do not believe that markets work: the Cubans, the North Koreans, and active managers.
> – Rex Sinquefield
> Dimensional Fund Advisors

Many mutual funds are also great offenders when it comes to tax-efficiency, even when they are held for longer periods of time. Since the average mutual fund trades the dollar equivalent of its entire holdings every year, even passive (buy-and-hold) fund investors may be hit with large tax bills at the end of each year. It is entirely possible for investors to have tax bills that exceed a fund's total return for the same period. By comparison, most index exchange-traded funds (ETFs) charge minimal fees and have virtually no tax impact before you liquidate, at which time you will likely pay the long-term capital gains tax rate. Much of the growth in index ETFs takes place in a "financial hot-house" unimpeded by the drag of taxes and compounding expenses.

When one looks at the big picture of sector rotation, fees, taxes, and the improbability of predicting the future, there is but one conclusion to be drawn. The best strategy is one that gains the broadest exposure to all industries and has the smallest possible fees, expenses, and tax implications. The one strategy that fits this description best is long-term index investing.

RVW Principle 5: *Protect Your Financial Core Through Diversification*

One of the greatest challenges faced by investors is portfolio construction. Everyone knows that a person should never put all of his or her eggs into one basket. The question remains: *How many eggs into how many baskets?* Diversification is the spreading of risk among multiple assets, and it works well to decrease the likelihood of loss in a portfolio to any one particular factor. Nevertheless, wise portfolio construction requires a real understanding of the risk versus reward of each particular investment and the relationships between investments. A properly constructed portfolio will include elements that move in opposite directions (negatively correlated) as well as independently of each other (noncorrelated).

> You can get your diversity and beat almost every single mutual fund manager simply by buying a stock index fund.
> – Jim Cramer, Host
> CNBC's *Mad Money*

Probably the simplest–and certainly the wisest–approach to this quandary is the "Core & Satellite" model of investing. The investor should identify what portion of his portfolio he can afford to lose and what portion is necessary for his long-term financial survival. The "core" portion should be invested in long-term conservative strategies. The "satellite" portion can be used for a group of more aggressive, shorter-term, and opportunistic investing, especially if the satellite elements were independent from and unrelated to the core and to each other.

It goes without saying that the larger an investor's core, the smaller the impact of the satellite portion of the portfolio. Divorced from the powerful allure of getting rich quickly, any rational investor should be willing to embrace smaller investments in risky gambles in exchange for the peace of mind and safety net that a conservatively invested core provides.

RVW Principle 6: *Invest Right. Then Sleep Tight.*®

The final, and perhaps most essential, principle of **RVW Investing** is to go to sleep. Although it sounds simple, it is, in all likelihood, the most difficult principle to apply. In fact, it is completely counterintuitive and contradictory to everything we know about life and human nature. The key element is learning to overcome the impulse to react. You will likely be facing regular bouts of either greed or fear–and your task is to ignore them both. It takes discipline and serious belief in the veracity of the conclusions of countless objective studies.

Any accomplished person knows that consistent professional success depends primarily on hard work. Scientists sift through data to prove their convictions. Many entrepreneurs rely on highly refined instincts and inspiration to make bold business moves. In the same way, soldiers are well-trained to immediately respond to danger. Even animals in the jungle instinctively react to threats with a fight-or-flight response.

> There are two times when a man shouldn't speculate: when he can't afford it, and when he can.
>
> – Mark Twain, Author
> *Following the Equator*

These deeply ingrained attitudes and behaviors are actually counter-productive to investing. For example, investors tend to sell stocks after a big drop, when the pain is no longer bearable. Generally speaking, investors are destined to sell at the worst time . . . right before an upward price reversal. On the other hand, they will often buy after they see a stock's price shoot up, not wanting to miss out on the upside, only to catch the ensuing downward correction. Analysts will pour over mountains of data and make determinations that are outdated simply because they rely on the changing circumstances. Simply put, the cards are stacked against us and we are hard-wired to do the wrong things at the wrong time.

RVW Investing is scientific and disciplined, and there is no room for reacting to gut feelings or intuition. *RVW investors* transcend the feebleness of all-too-human investing behavior. They know from the outset that their portfolio will go up and down over time. They understand clearly that the stock market is like a man walking up stairs while playing with a yo-yo. Over the long term, it is completely irrelevant whether the yo-yo goes up or down because his feet are always climbing–**the key is to watch the feet and not the yo-yo**. The RVW approach is so simple, so straight forward, and so validated by the empirical evidence, that all a rational investor ever needs to do is: *Invest right. Then sleep Tight.*®

The Underpinnings of the RVW Approach: Why It Works

In 1900, a Frenchman named Louis Bachelier published a thesis called *Theory of Speculation*. In his work, Bachelier concluded that stock market prices follow a "random walk" in which historic price trends have no predictable influence on future price movement. Six decades later, the "efficient-market" hypothesis finally began to gain widespread acceptance in academic circles. Paul A. Samuelson, the famous neoclassical economist, brought renewed attention to Bachelier's seminal paper, and Eugene F. Fama tested the theory against actual US market data. Fama's findings supported Bachelier's thesis: *An investor learns no useful information about likely future stock market prices by examining past performance.*

> Here's a simple, effective way to lower your anxiety: Investors who perceived the least risk were those who checked their investments no more than once a year.
>   – Richard Thaler, Economist

Fundamental analysis, technical analysis, i.e., stock charting, industry insight, and all the other esoteric Wall Street techniques for predicting stock price movements are demonstrably worthless. This theory was advanced significantly and began to gain widespread acceptance after Burton G. Malkiel, a Wall Street banker turned Princeton professor, published his classic work, *A Random Walk Down Wall Street*. Malkiel refined the "efficient-market hypothesis," showing how prices of publicly traded assets reflect all available information. Predicting stock price movements is, therefore, a futile attempt to forecast randomness. "The true news is random," says Malkiel. "That's what people had trouble grasping. It's not that stock prices are capricious. It's that the news is capricious." This hypothesis is at the heart of the RVW approach and it is our academic gospel. It is the reason over $1 trillion of assets has moved out of stock-picking, mutual funds, and active portfolio management . . . and found its way into passive, index-based exchange-traded funds.

In the few pages to this point, I have outlined the indisputable facts. The remaining question is: *"How do we deal with them and respond within our investment portfolios?"*

> Facts are stubborn things.
>   – Rip Van Winkle Wisdom

Fama's explanation is simple: Higher returns are always the compensation for taking on risk. The stock market offers higher returns than the bond market only because it is more volatile. Likewise, the higher risk of small-cap stocks will manifest itself in rewarding the investor with higher returns. All other information about future market movements Fama dismisses as "noise." As for those investors who systematically beat the market, Fama insists they simply don't exist. If millions of monkeys throw darts at *The Wall Street Journal* stock pages, at least a few of them would pick a group of winning stocks.

Our chief task, then, as RVW investors, is to ignore the noise and distractions which Wall Street regularly dispenses. Suppressing our natural instincts to follow the crowd and listen to the "experts" is our greatest challenge. The RVW office has no TVs or automated trading screens running, no Bloomberg terminals, and no frenetic traders. It is a calm and disciplined place.

There's a pile of discarded financial bestsellers once found on the bookshelves like: Ravi Batra's *The Great Depression of 1990*; Harry Dent's *The Roaring 2000s*; James Glassman's *Dow 36,000*; Harry Figgie's *Bankruptcy 1995: The Coming Collapse of America and How to Stop It*. There is also *BusinessWeek's* 1979 description of "the death of equities as a near permanent condition," and *SmartMoney's* cover story, "Seven Best Mutual Funds for 1996"–picks that went on to underperform the market by nearly 7%. In 1997, *SmartMoney* again selected the seven "best" mutual fund managers. As a group, they finished 3.4% below the broad market index. In 1998, the magazine's list of "best funds" came in 2.2% below the market. Soon thereafter, *SmartMoney* ceased publishing these annual surveys.

> In theory, there is no difference between theory and practice. In practice there is.
> – Yogi Berra

Diversification Is a Major Benefit of Investing in Exchange-Traded Funds

Company or individual security risk is the risk that a specific stock may fall in price due to non-market-related factors such as poor company management. It is the risk in excess of the overall stock market and is not always rewarded with higher returns. You assume greater *company risk* when you invest in a limited number of securities.

Including more securities in a portfolio can reduce the level of company-specific risk to which you are exposed. This is true for stocks as well as other types of asset classes. This image illustrates that an investor holding more than one hundred stocks assumes little company risk.

Generally, it is impractical for most investors to buy hundreds of individual stocks. Both ETFs and mutual funds are able to reduce company risk because they have economies of scale. Both types of funds often take positions in hundreds of stocks.

Even ETFs and mutual funds, however, cannot diversify away market risk. Market risk is the possibility that the entire market will experience a decline in price. Even if you hold every stock in the market and have very little company-specific risk, you will still be exposed to market risk. Market declines can be entirely unrelated to the actual performance of the companies whose stocks are declining in value.

Likewise, diversification does not entirely eliminate the risk of experiencing investment losses. Returns and principal invested in stocks are not guaranteed, and mutual funds have management fees and other additional costs. An investment cannot be made directly in an index.

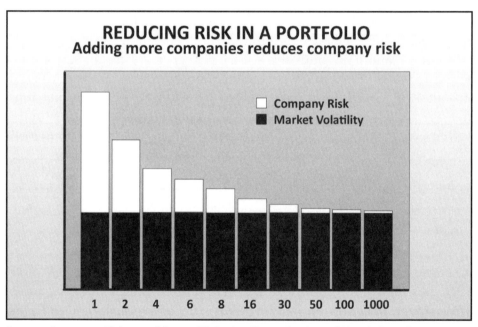

Sources: Lawrence Fisher and James H. Lorie, "Some Studies of Variability of Returns on Investments in Common Stocks," *Journal of Business*, April 1970; Edwin J. Elton and Martin J. Gruber, "Risk Reduction and Portfolio Size: An Analytical Solution," *Journal of Business*, October 1977; and Meir Statman, "How Many Stocks Make a Diversified Portfolio?," *Journal of Financial and Quantitative Analysis*, September 1987.

In the pages that follow, you will discover for yourself that, despite the slick, Madison Avenue-created marketing materials that promote stocks, bonds, and mutual funds for Wall Street brokerages, fund managers, and others, a relatively benign approach to investing–we call it *RVW Investing*– over the long term will generally outperform the most talented stock-pickers, market-timing gurus, and the "financial experts" the TV news talking heads turn to for their "analysis" every time the markets move up or down.

> Rip Van Winkle [is the] style of investing that we favor. Our stay-put behavior reflects our view that the stock market serves as a relocation center at which money is moved from the active to the patient. The much maligned idle rich have received a bad rap: They have maintained or increased their wealth while many of the energetic rich have seen their fortunes disappear.
>
> – Warren E. Buffett
> *Letter to Investors*, March 24, 1992

The Essential Levels of RVW Investing

LEVEL 1: INDEXING BEATS ACTIVE MANAGEMENT

Most investors can do this on their own far better than being a victim of the Wall Street marketing machine disguised as "financial advice."

LEVEL 2: ENHANCED STRATEGIC INDEXING BEATS CAP-WEIGHTED INDEXING

Most investors will not persevere relentlessly in the pursuit of a well-maintained portfolio and fall short of the returns to which they are entitled. Partnering with *RVW Investing* can overcome this.

LEVEL 3: ASSET ALLOCATION IS THE PRIMARY DETERMINANT OF PORTFOLIO PERFORMANCE

Many investors understand the need to allocate their portfolio, but lack the confidence to do so on their own. They turn to others perceived as "professionals" for "advice" and usually give up something of greater value in the process–long-term performance.

It comes as no surprise that, when placing bonds in their portfolio, given all the misunderstanding of US tax law, too many investors hold tax-free municipal bonds for their perceived efficiencies. Based on their specific income tax situations, many are literally robbing themselves of superior returns available from taxable bonds.

When investors partner with *RVW Investing*, we assist them by monitoring ratings and optimizing the selection of tax-free and taxable bonds in every portfolio. Those exposed to the Alternative Minimum Tax need to be especially vigilant. We also have access to a broad selection of bonds at more favorable institutional pricing.

	Real Estate Stocks	High-Yield Bonds	Emerging-Market Stocks	Investment-Grade Bonds	Small-Cap Stocks	Value Stocks	Growth Stocks	Large-Cap Stocks	Foreign Developed-Country Stocks	Commodities
2010	19.1	11.8	11.0	10.5	9.1	4.8	4.8	3.9	1.5	-3.9
2009	79.0	57.5	37.0	32.5	28.0	27.2	26.5	19.8	13.5	5.9
2008	5.2	-26.4	-33.8	-36.3	-37.0	-37.7	-38.4	-43.1	-46.5	-53.2
2007	39.8	32.7	11.6	1.4	7.0	5.5	2.2	-1.0	-1.6	-15.7
2006	35.1	32.6	26.9	22.3	18.4	15.8	11.8	9.5	4.3	2.4
2005	34.5	25.6	14.0	12.2	6.9	5.2	4.9	4.6	2.7	2.4
2004	31.6	26.0	20.7	18.3	17.3	16.9	10.9	10.9	6.9	4.3
2003	56.3	47.3	39.2	37.1	31.1	31.0	28.7	28.1	20.7	4.1
2002	32.1	10.3	3.8	-1.9	-6.0	-15.2	-15.7	-20.5	-22.4	-28.0
2001	13.9	8.4	4.5	2.5	-2.4	-4.3	-11.9	-19.6	-22.4	-31.9
2000	49.7	26.4	11.6	8.0	-3.0	-5.1	-9.1	-14.0	-22.4	-30.6
1999	66.4	40.9	33.8	27.3	21.3	21.0	6.7	2.5	-0.8	-4.6
1998	35.0	28.6	20.3	13.5	8.7	3.0	-2.5	-17.5	-25.3	-35.7
1997	34.8	33.4	28.7	22.4	20.3	13.3	9.7	2.1	-11.6	-14.4
1996	35.3	33.9	23.0	21.9	21.6	16.5	11.3	6.4	6.0	3.6
1995	37.6	37.0	36.6	28.4	20.5	20.3	18.5	15.3	11.6	-5.2
1994	8.1	5.3	3.2	2.2	1.3	-1.0	-1.8	-1.9	-2.9	-7.3
1993	74.8	32.9	19.7	18.9	18.7	16.7	10.1	9.7	3.7	-12.3
1992	18.4	17.4	14.9	14.6	11.4	7.6	7.4	5.2	4.4	-11.8
1991	59.9	46.1	41.7	39.2	35.7	30.5	25.4	16.0	12.5	-6.1
1990	29.1	9.0	-1.3	-3.1	-4.4	-8.8	-10.6	-15.4	-19.5	-23.2
1989	65.0	38.3	34.7	31.7	24.2	16.3	14.5	10.8	8.8	2.3
1988	40.4	28.6	27.9	25.0	23.6	16.6	13.5	13.4	12.0	7.9

*As of 9/30/2010. Asset classes represented by: Large Caps – S&P 500 Index; Small Caps – Russell 2000 Index; Growth – Russell 3000 Growth Index; Value – Russell 3000 Value Index; Developed Country Stocks – MSCI EAFE Index; Emerging Markets – MSCI Emerging Markets Index; High Yield – Bank of America Merrill Lynch U.S. High Yield Index; Investment-Grade Bonds – Barclays Capital U.S. Aggregate Bond Index; Real Estate – NAREIT Equity-Only Index; Commodities – S&P GSCI Commodity Index. Source: Ibbotson Associates, Standard and Poor's, Haver Analytics, FMRCo (MARE) as of 9/30/10. Past performance is no guarantee of future results.

Source: RVW Research

This chart represents the best performing asset classes each year for the past 20 years. It demonstrates that just because an asset class performed well in a previous year does not mean it will do well again.

Chapter 1
Laziness Pays

> The great error in Rip's composition was an insuperable aversion to all kinds of profitable labor . . . . In a word, Rip was ready to attend to anybody's business but his own; but as to doing family duty, and keeping his farm in order, he found it impossible.
> – Washington Irving, Author
> *The Sketch Book of Geoffrey Crayon, Gent.*

Stocks can provide steady, long-term gains. Investment success is a triumph of discipline over emotion and results from ignoring the short-term fluctuations in order to reap gains over time.

Rip Van Winkle is not a man unwilling to engage the world. Rather, he is a man whose very disposition is contrary to preoccupation with worldly affairs. While he is always willing to lend a hand and help a friend in need, he has no concern for maximizing every opportunity to advance his own pecuniary interests. It is this quality of having minimal concern for his own gains, more than any other, which would have saved him from the mistakes made by typical investors each and every day.

> Rip Van Winkle would be the ideal stock market investor. Rip could invest in the market before his nap and when he woke up 20 years later, he'd be happy. He would have been asleep through all the ups and downs in between.
> – Richard Thaler, Economist

In order to understand why this is true, an individual must understand the difference between long-term and short-term market behavior and the critical errors made by most investors that stifle returns. All too often, investors inadvertently make short-term decisions that have a significant and adverse impact on their long-term wealth.

Bulls, Bears, and Other Hairy Creatures

The theoretical formula for stock market success is quite simple and universally known: *BUY LOW, SELL HIGH*. The devil, so to speak, is in the details. How do we know when prices are low or high? Anybody who has bought a stock knows that the value of every stock has the potential to either increase or decrease. In fact, the typical investor does the exact opposite of what he or she should do: buying when stock prices are high and selling when they are low. Why this is so will be discussed in later chapters.

If blessed with perfect omniscience, an investor will always know when to get into a market and when to get out. He will be fully invested when prices are rising in a "bull" market and will hold cash when prices are falling in a "bear" market. The problem in the short term is that we can watch the bulls wrestle the bears, but we can rarely see definitively who is winning. As soon as it seems certain that the bears are in control, the market can violently turn in the other direction. The confirmation of a trend often comes too late, just as market forces are about to spiral in the opposite direction.

> If I have noticed anything over these 60 years on Wall Street, it is that people do not succeed in forecasting what's going to happen to the stock market.
>
>   – Benjamin Graham, Author
>   *Security Analysis*
>   (Mentor to Warren Buffett)

On the other hand, the long-term picture, seen in Figure 1-2, is quite different. Simply put, growth in the market represents the underlying growth in the economy. As economies expand, so do the earnings of those companies that make up the lion's share of economic activity. While at any given time economic expectations will cause markets to misvalue stock prices relative to earnings, earnings growth is the truest indicator of value creation. The conclusion is obvious: Over the short term there will be bear markets from time to time, but history is always, ultimately, on the side of the bulls.

The long-term results of equity investing indicate that you can ignore all the predictions of recessions, depressions to rival the 1930s, or runaway inflation. *Individual stocks may sizzle and then fizzle, but in the long run, the major indexes always regain their lost ground and move ahead.* In Figure 1-3, we map every market decline of at least 10 percent that has occurred since the end of World War II. These declines have averaged ten months in duration and took thirteen months to recover from an average decline of approximately 22%.

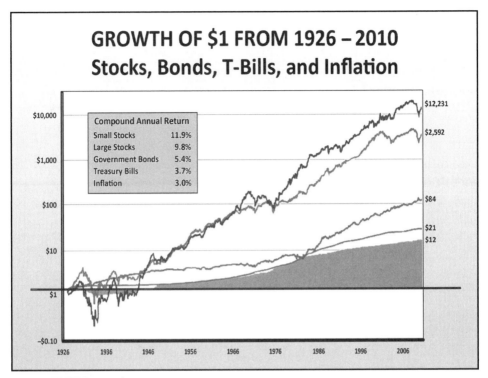

GROWTH OF $1 FROM 1926 – 2010
Stocks, Bonds, T-Bills, and Inflation

Compound Annual Return	
Small Stocks	11.9%
Large Stocks	9.8%
Government Bonds	5.4%
Treasury Bills	3.7%
Inflation	3.0%

Source: RVW Research

Figure 1-1: While bond returns underperform stocks in the long run, they usually do best during those time periods when stocks perform the worst.

Bear Markets Always End

> A bear market is simply a tightly coiled spring ready to bounce.
> – Rip Van Winkle Wisdom

And what about the big, bad bear? Bear markets are nothing to fear–they have happened before and they are a normal and necessary part of the markets' cycles. Events like the 1929 crash, the oil crisis of the 1970s, the 1989 savings and loan crisis, Long-term Capital Management's bailout in 1998, the "dot.com" crash of 2000, the 9/11 attacks in 2001, and the 2008-2009 banking and real estate crisis each had an immediate impact. Yet each time the market fell back, it soon resumed its steady move forward (Figure 1-1). Sadly, most investors failed to share in this experience because they chose active management over strategic, index-based investing.

The Case for Indexing: Debunking the Active Management Myth

Index-based investing is backed by Nobel laureate economists who have provided unbiased, rigorous, empirical analysis. Their research, and that of others, shows that over any ten-year period, at least 80% of active managers and mutual funds underperform their benchmarks (pp. 153-154). It is also an astounding fact that portfolios selected by throwing darts routinely outperform the professionals' selections (p. 32). While individual stock-picking is like looking for a needle in a haystack, **with index investing you buy the haystack.**

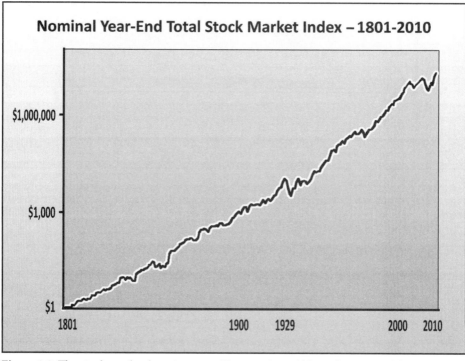

Figure 1-2: The stock market has risen steadily over time. Although gains and losses appear to be greater on the right side of the chart, that is only because the value of this widely followed average has gotten higher over time. The decline which occurred in 1929 was much worse, on a percentage basis, than the recent bear market that began in 2000. Viewed from a long-term perspective, neither was as bad as investors feared at the time.

Tax Savings and Cost Savings

Active investors pay substantial transaction costs and management fees. Profits tend to be taxed when earned, and at higher ordinary income tax rates. Index funds, on the other hand, tend to be very efficient since they aren't bearing these heavy costs of management and there are no high-paid Wall Street-types involved. In addition, there are far fewer transactions, so gains accumulate tax-deferred over long periods of time, and when they are ultimately taxed it's at far lower, long-term, capital gains rates.

A Dynamic, Self-Selecting Group of Winners

Of the original thirty companies included in the Dow Jones in 1926, only three companies have survived into the twenty-first century. In these rapidly changing times, identifying which companies–if any–will survive into the future is more difficult than ever. Diversification is a cornerstone of a sound investment strategy. Investing in an index reduces the risk that any individual company's failure will adversely impact performance. You always own a piece of the best-of-breed companies in each category.

> Investment policy (asset allocation) is the foundation upon which portfolios should be constructed and managed.
> – Charles D. Ellis, Author

Market-Timing Doesn't Work

Research indicates that most of this strong, long-term upward thrust occurs during surprisingly short intervals. In fact, nearly all of the market's total return over this eighty-four-year period took place in a total of just forty months, and in 2010, the entire gain of 15% in the major indexes was earned in just the best six trading days of the year. Index-based investing ensures that the investor is exposed to these strong but brief spurts. The cost of not being invested during these surges is almost always far greater than the cost of being invested during a cyclical bear market. A recent study reviewed performance of the thirty-two leading market-timing newsletters and found that not one had beaten the S&P 500® over a ten-year period.

What About Bonds?

Looking back at Figure 1-1 again, you can see that the total returns generated by bonds pale in comparison to those of stocks. Bonds are best for short-term needs–they're contractually obligated to pay interest regularly and repay principal on a given date so you have certainty of income and principal. Since the interest rates are fixed, the real enemy of bondholders is inflation, and the longer the time to maturity, the worse bond returns look. And this is precisely why bonds and equities in a portfolio work so well in combination–equities really shine over the long term.

One question investors often ask is whether or not their investments will keep up with inflation. The answer to this is a resounding, "Yes!" and is clearly seen in the trends in Figure 1-2.

To be certain, inflation does diminish the future value of a dollar, yet both the stock and bond markets do a very nice job of mitigating the impact. As Figure 1-1 shows, although bonds are far more severely impacted, the gains from investing in either stocks or bonds over eighty-four years easily surpass the cumulative effect of inflation.

Following a RVW investment strategy, you will insulate yourself against the three most common pitfalls of investing:

1. Waiting for the "perfect" time to buy.

2. Chasing last year's winners (which is like driving down the road while looking in the rear-view mirror).

3. Panicking during market volatility (which usually results in selling securities at a loss).

Instead, you will own a piece of thousands of successful businesses in a variety of groupings, and, most importantly, you will sleep peacefully for twenty years or longer.

INVESTING IN BONDS	
THE GOOD	Predictable returns, certainty of principal repayment
THE BAD	Returns tend to be substantially below equities
THE UGLY	Inflation will shrink the real value of both the principal invested and the income

The RVW Investment Strategy Has Built-In Insulation

Most people, however, do not invest all at once. For example, many contribute small pieces of their earnings each year to their Individual Retirement Arrangement (IRA) to build a nest egg for the future. Fortunately, the picture is even better for those investors who invest their earnings on a systematic basis over time.

One method of systematic investing, known as *Dollar-Cost Averaging*, leads to those long-term gains and helps to smooth out the violent zigs and zags that come hand-in-hand with lump sum investing. While this method may not be right for all investors, the graph in Figure 1-1 shows the tremendous power of a long-term buy-and-hold strategy that ignores short-term fluctuations in market prices.

Unfortunately investors rarely see the forest for the trees, and short-term market volatility scares many investors out of the stock market. This usually occurs when things look their worst, and right before the long-term upward trend reasserts itself. RVW investors, however, won't even notice these swings as they will be sleeping well and enjoying their lives, confident of the long-term outcome rather than anxiously watching every market tick.

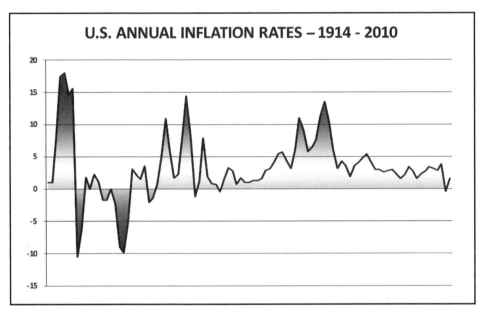

Source: US Bureau of Labor Statistics & RVW Research

Figure 1-4: The purchasing power of $100 in 1914 would require about $2,269 in 2011, an increase of *nearly 2,169%*. Inflation periodically spikes but only rarely goes negative. Smart investors need to plan for inflation, but history shows they will maintain the ability to fund their lifestyle simply by remaining invested. Figure 1-1 demonstrates the value stock and bond investments have provided to their purchasers as a hedge against inflation when held for long periods of time.

In order to enjoy these long-term gains from the stock market, you simply need to be in the market. That means you need to stick with stocks through both the good times and the bad. Remember, first of all, that the returns shown in Figure 1-2 were amassed over more than 200 years (1801-2010), and included World War I ("the war to end all wars"), the stock market crash of 1929 and the ensuing Great Depression, World War II, and the more than forty years of the Cold War. And these are not the only crises and crashes. The Dow Jones Industrial Average lost more than 22% *in a single day* in October 1987, and the NASDAQ Composite Index fell almost 80% in the months after the Internet bubble burst. The stock market, throughout its history, has gone through cycles of boom and bust. While no one has yet successfully predicted the peaks and troughs, these can be seen in hindsight, and are nevertheless instructive for investors.

A Sidebar Discussion on Inflation

No discussion on investing should dance around the topic of inflation. After all, it is precisely being invested that helps to insulate the investor from the ill effects of inflation *over the long term.*

In periods of "normal" inflation (when inflation is running at 3%-5% annually), stocks have proven to be the bellwether. Bond prices also fare better when inflation and interest rates are on the wane. In periods of runaway inflation, however, as we experienced from the mid-1970s to the mid-1980s, both domestic stocks and all manner of bonds will be negatively impacted *in the short-term.*

> Inflation is the insidious, though technically legal, way in which the government defaults on its obligations.
>
> – Professor Jeremy J. Siegel

Writing in the June 2011 issue of *Kiplinger Personal Finance,* Jeremy Siegel shared his concerns about the threat to investors resulting from the combination of the US government's fiscal policies that have led to massive debt and the "easy" monetary policies of the Federal Reserve Board, both of which he views as inflationary. According to Siegel, as long as there is not a return to double-digit inflation, stocks will provide an excellent hedge against inflation:

> Stocks are claims on real assets, such as real estate, plant and equipment, trademarks, intellectual property, inventories and natural resources, which appreciate in value when inflation causes prices to rise. Most companies can flow through increased costs and pass them onto their customers, thus further insulating the portfolio against the effects of inflation. The larger enterprises have international operations and therefore also provide safeguards against a falling dollar because the value of their foreign assets and income increase in dollar terms as the dollar loses value.

Illustrating the Power of Compounding

To fully comprehend the power of a buy and hold strategy, one must understand the principle of compounding returns. Simply put, compounding is when the principal for each period's return is calculated as the previous period's principal added to its growth. For example, if Joe invests $100 at a 10% rate of return, he will have $110 at the end of year one. In year two, he will earn 10% on that $110, or $11, and his account will be worth $121, and so on. The more time our money has to grow, the wealthier we become as the result of this simple principle.

To illustrate the power of compounding, imagine twenty-one-year-old Susan who makes a one-time $5,000 contribution to her Roth IRA. If her coworker David waits, instead, to contribute the same $5,000 to a Roth IRA when he is thirty-one, he will retire with a nest egg 60% smaller than the one Susan created with her $5,000 contribution made just ten years earlier.

Because of the "magic" of compounding, Susan saves two-and-a-half times more for her retirement in only ten years. In this example, we have assumed that both Roth IRAs earned an average annual return of 10%, a little less than the NYSE has delivered in its history.

Both savers in our example want to be responsible and begin saving for their retirement, but they achieve dramatically different results. While each accumulates substantial wealth, one allows her money to work harder by starting earlier. This is explained by the **Rule of 72**, which is a general mathematical formula that investors can use to figure out approximately how long it will take for their money to double at any given rate of return.

The Rule says you can divide the number 72 by any rate of return to find out how about long it takes for money to double at that interest rate. For example if you earn 10% on your money, it would double in about 7.2 years (72 ÷ 10 = 7.2). Compounding assumes, of course, that you keep all of your investment in place in order to earn interest on both the principal and all of the accumulated gains ("total return").

Perhaps the earliest reference to the Rule of 72 appeared in 1494 in Luca Pacioli's *Summa de Arithmetica*, but it is believed that the Rule was known even earlier than that. Physicist Albert Einstein once called it "the greatest mathematical discovery of all time."

Looking again at our example of the two Roth IRA investors in Table 1-2, when both are age sixty-one, with only six years to go until retirement, the investor who started saving when she was twenty-one has more than $226,286 in her account. The investor who started ten years later has just $87,247 in his. Over the next six years, each account will nearly double;

obviously it's better to double a larger sum of money. Saving early gives your money as much time as possible to work for you. And saving more on a regular basis means having much more accumulated savings over time.

The Story of Two Savers

Saver A spends his money partying for 8 years, then opens a tax-deferred account earning 12% at age 26 and invests $150/Month for the next 40 years

Contributions = $72,000

Saver B invests $150/Month for 8 years in a tax-deferred account earning 12% and saves NOTHING for the next 40 years

Contributions = $14,400

Which saver ends up with more money?

	Saver A			Saver B	
Age	Annual Amt	Total	Age	Annual Amt	Total
18	$0	$0	18	$1,800	$1,902
19	0	0	19	1,800	4,046
20	0	0	20	1,800	6,462
21	0	0	21	1,800	9,183
22	0	0	22	1,800	12,250
23	0	0	23	1,800	15,706
24	0	0	24	1,800	19,600
25	0	0	25	1,800	23,989
26	1,800	1,902	26	0	26,868
27	1,800	4,046	27	0	30,092
28	1,800	6,462	28	0	33,703
29	1,800	9,183	29	0	37,747
30	1,800	12,250	30	0	42,277
35	1,800	34,506	35	0	74,506
40	1,800	74,937	40	0	131,305
45	1,800	148,388	45	0	231,405
50	1,800	281,827	50	0	407,815
55	1,800	524,245	55	0	718,709
60	1,800	964,644	60	0	1,266,610
65	1,800	1,764,716	65	0	2,232,200

Saver B invests only 20% as much as Saver A, but accumulates over $467,000 more than Saver A!

Don't Procrastinate!

Source: JeremySeigel.com & RVW Research

Figure 1-5. The Rule of 72 in action. Saving early is the most important factor.

AGE	SAVINGS BEGINNING AT 21	SAVINGS BEGINNING AT 31
21	$5,000	$0
31	$12,968.71	$5,000
41	$33,637.50	$12,968.71
51	$87,247.01	$33,637.50
61	$226,296.28	$87,247.01
67	$400,897.66	$154,563.40

Table 1-2: Note the differences due to the age when savings begin. The longer you allow your money to work for you, the greater your accumulation of wealth.

Don't Look for Needles; Buy the Haystack

We now know that, historically, stock markets have always recovered from their lows, only to reach new highs. While this is definitely true of stock markets, sadly, it is untrue of individual stocks. In a free market economy, some companies stand the test of time, while others disappear from the face of the earth, never to return.

Selecting the winners and avoiding the losers is the chief focus of building an actively managed portfolio, but doing so is easier said than done. Of the three surviving companies out of twelve included in the original Dow Jones Industrial Average created in 1896, only General Electric remains one of its thirty constituents today.

THE PERILS OF STOCK MARKET PREDICTING

Wall Street strategists say the Standard & Poor's 500 Index will post the biggest fourth-quarter rally in 13 years. The benchmark index for U.S. stocks will climb 14 percent to end 2011 at 1,300, according to the average estimate of 12 strategists surveyed by Bloomberg. The last time they were this bullish in October was 2008, when the group predicted a 27 percent gain and the index lost 18 percent.

– *Bloomberg News*, October 6, 2011

The more stocks we own, however, the less vulnerable our portfolios are to the catastrophic decline of any individual company. Through "diversification" we are able to spread the risk throughout our portfolio. While this technique may also mute any dramatic upward movement of any individual stocks, the portfolio as a whole will reflect the steady, upward grind of its components. Without question, diversification is the cornerstone of a sound investment strategy.

The most powerful method of diversification is not to own individual stocks at all, but to own the whole market, or segments of it, through "reflective indexing."

The Added Value of Noncorrelated Investing

Although the most well-known indexes are the Dow Jones 30 and the S&P 500®, they each cover only the largest companies in America. There are indexes for many distinct groupings within the market. For example, there are indexes for mid-sized and small companies, and the smaller companies frequently perform far better than the larger ones. Over 50% of global equities are now located outside the USA–and trade on the bourses of Europe, Japan, and Australia, and in the emerging and frontier markets. Each of those has an index fund associated with it.

There are also indexes to reflect commodities and resources such as gold, oil, and metals. In addition to providing the safety of additional diversification, these sub-markets frequently move independently of each other, thus providing insulation from excessive volatility. For example, in 2000 the S&P 500® Index declined by 9.1% while the Russell 2000 Value Index–which includes smaller, asset-heavy companies–grew by 22.8%. For the decade ending in 2010, the S&P 500® essentially delivered minimal returns while small-cap and mid-cap companies generated attractive annual rates of return in the 6%–8% range.

> 'Tis the part of a wise man to keep himself today for tomorrow, and not to venture all his eggs in one basket.
> – Miguel de Cervantes, Author
> *Don Quixote*

Index-based investing ensures that the investor is exposed to those strong, but brief, spurts that deliver most of the gains. The cost of being out of the market during these surges is almost always far greater than the cost of being in the market during the decline of a cyclical bear market. Although many believe that they can time the markets, avoiding the declines while participating in the gains, research shows this to be a near-impossible task. A recent study reviewed the performance of thirty-two leading market-timing newsletters and found that not one had beaten the S&P 500® over a ten-year period!

Index investing has become easier than ever with the proliferation of Exchange-Traded Funds (ETFs). Although first created in 1993, and largely overlooked by investors prior to the bear market of 2000-2002, ETFs are primarily index funds that trade just like stocks on exchanges around the world, in real time, and typically carry lower embedded fees than most mutual funds. ETFs are the least expensive, easiest, and most efficient way to invest in indexes. It's a complete wonder that they have not yet become the cornerstone of the typical investor's portfolio.

> A blindfolded monkey throwing darts at a newspaper's financial pages could select a portfolio that would do just as well as one carefully selected by experts.
> – Burton G. Malkiel, Economist and Author
> *A Random Walk Down Wall Street*

Through sound index-based investing and smart asset allocation, you should enjoy steady, long-term, market-beating returns. Using index funds, you will own pieces of the most successful businesses in a variety of sectors. You'll also be able to enjoy some exposure to inflation hedges such as natural resources and commodities. Bonds round out the portfolio by providing predictable income and decreased volatility.

Contest 37: Darts Lead the Readers

With a little over two weeks remaining in Investment Dartboard Contest 37, the stocks picked by darts thrown by Sunday Journal staffers at stock tables are up an average 27% since Sept. 30, compared with the 11% decline of the readers' picks.

READER PICKS (-11%)	PURCHASE PRICE 9/30/09	PRICE 3/10/10	CHANGE SINCE 9/30/09
Corrections Corp. of America (CXW)	$22.65	$21.07	-7%
Gary Wurtz, Arizona Daily Star			
Energy Conversion Devices (ENER)	11.58	8.04	-31
Ralph Louks, Flint Journal			
Fuel Systems Solutions (FSYS)	35.99	31.10	-14
Robert Falcon, Providence Journal			
General Electric (GE)	16.42	16.51	+0.5
Anna Marie Colonnese, Port St. Lucie News			
ON Semiconductor (ONNN)	8.25	8.27	+0.2
Patrick Jamison, Winston-Salem Journal			
Sigma Designs (SIGM)	14.53	12.28	-16
Roy Parfitt, News Tribute (Tacoma, Wash.)			

DARTS (+27%)	PURCHASE PRICE 9/30/09	PRICE 3/10/10	CHANGE SINCE 9/30/09
Avocent (AVCT**)	$20.27	$24.99	+23
Bally Technologies (BYI)	38.37	38.44	+0.2
Concho resources (CXO)	36.37	49.53	+36
Cullen/Frost Bankers (CFR)	51.64	55.21	+7
Harte-Hanks (HHS)	13.83	12.35	-12
UAL (UAUA)	9.22	18.98	+106

** Last trade was $24.99. Effective Dec 11, 2009, Avocent become a wholly owned subsidiary of Emerson Electric and is no longer a publicly traded company.

Source: *The Wall Street Journal Sunday* (December 13, 2009)

Figure 1-6: Stock-picking readers of the *Sunday Journal* fared horribly against the *Journal*'s own dart-throwing staffers in 2009. The readers fared slightly better in 2010 but did not manage to beat the returns for the *Journal*'s randomly selected stocks for the year. In most prior years, the random selections made, literally, by tossing darts at the stock pages consistently beat the professional stock-pickers and the "educated" picks of *Journal* readers.

When you see a line outside a department store, it is reasonable to assume that there is a sale. When you see a crowd of investors herding, it is usually more Nostradumbus than Nostradamus.

– Rip Van Winkle Wisdom

Chapter 2
Hard Work–The Myths and the Math

In fact, he declared it was of no use to work on his farm; it was the most pestilent little piece of ground in the whole country; every thing about it went wrong, and would go wrong, in spite of him.

— Washington Irving, Author
Rip Van Winkle

Most people think successful investing requires hard work. It is not surprising that we think this, given the fact that success generally requires effort and diligence. Large numbers of market participants devote a huge amount of time and energy to active trading, attempting to time the market in order to select winning stocks out of a sea of losers. Others pore through hundreds of mutual fund prospectuses attempting to find managers who will beat the market. We will see in this chapter that the great majority of this hard work is in vain.

Can Hard Work Predict Market Moves?

Many investors believe it is within their power to buy stocks low and sell them high. This impression is nurtured by the stories they read about master traders who have successfully parlayed modest initial capital into billions of dollars. If only they could learn the "secrets" to successful trading or market timing, they, too, could partake of this interminable reservoir of potential wealth.

A simple math challenge drives home the allure of this tempting path. Nobel Prize-winning economist Robert Merton looked at what would happen if an expert timer correctly predicted the market direction at the beginning of each month. An investor starting in 1927 with only $1,000, and holding stocks in up months and treasury bills in down months, would have earned more than $5.3 billion by 1978, compared to only $67,500 for a buy-and-hold investor.

In fact, a veritable cottage industry has sprung up of so-called trading and market-timing gurus hawking trading systems and market-timing newsletters that promise investors outsized returns. Simple logic should dissuade people from buying these products. If their advocates really did know the secrets to the market's mysteries, why would they sell them for $99 per subscription instead of using them to make billions for themselves? For those who cling to the false hope offered by these letters, the following data will provide a rude awakening.

> There are two kinds of forecasters. Those who don't know and those who don't know that they don't know.
> — John Kenneth Galbraith, Economist

Business professors from the University of Utah and Duke University collaborated in a detailed study of newsletter performance. Professors John Graham and Campbell Harvey tracked more than 15,000 recommendations made in 237 investment newsletters from the middle of 1980 through the end of 1992. Their first conclusion was that the life of a newsletter is usually fairly short–during that time 95% of the experts stopped publishing their newsletter after an average operating period of about four years. The other conclusion they reached is, "There is no evidence that newsletters can time the market."

Mark Hulbert publishes a service that independently tracks newsletter performance. He was able to find twenty-five newsletters that remained in business for the full ten-year period from 1988 through 1997. He found that these newsletters delivered an average annual return of 11.1%, which was seven full points less than the 18.1% average return of the S&P 500®.

The results from trading systems are often much worse than these newsletters. Purchasers of these systems rarely know the risks involved or have realistic expectations for their potential profits. Moreover, once transaction costs and taxes are added into the equation, these strategies become even more unattractive.

> Skepticism about past returns is crucial. The truth is, much as you may wish you could know which funds will be hot, you can't–and neither can the legions of advisors and publications that claim they can.
> — Bethany McLean, writer
> "The Skeptic's Guide to Mutual Funds"
> *Fortune*, March 15, 1999

Professional traders and market-timers are akin to professional gamblers (indeed, market-timing letters are hardly more instructive than the "sure thing" horse racing "reports" sold to bettors at the track). They play a difficult and dangerous game of risk management. Very few join the ranks of the *uber*-wealthy, while the others eventually crash and burn, losing billions in the process. Anybody who reads the financial pages has heard of the astounding losses of professional traders gone awry.

Amateur traders, on the other hand, are much like their Las Vegas counterparts. In their pursuit of great wealth, they often end up holding an empty bag. The only difference is that instead of building casinos on the strip, their losses go to building the towering skyscrapers of Wall Street. Or worse yet, they hand over their investable cash to a *Ponzi* schemer like Bernard Madoff, and their "profits" evaporate into offshore bank accounts.

Even the conservative market-timer, who is not making large bets with the desire to amass great wealth, is at a great disadvantage. By moving in and out of his positions, he is liable to miss dramatic upswings that come unannounced.

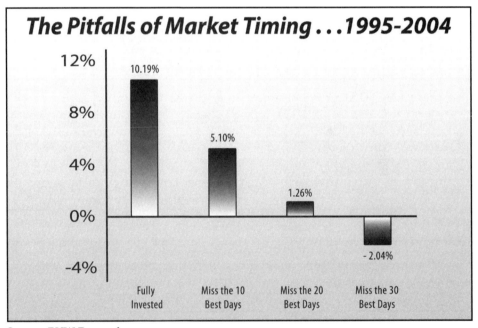

Source: RVW Research

Figure 2-1: Missing the best days in the market during the ten years ending in December 2004 would have resulted in lower returns than investing in Treasury Bills.

Another study, conducted by the investment management firm SEI, found that missing the ten best trading days in a ten-year period could result in losing out on nearly half of the gains available to the long-term investor. Looking at stocks from 1980 to 1989, they found that simply buying and doing nothing over the 2,528 trading days would have resulted in a 17.5% annualized return. Missing only the ten days with the largest gains lowered the return to 12.6% per year–and profits fell to only $22,763 instead of $40,162 on a $10,000 investment.

Another way of looking at this is shown in Figure 2-1. The ten years ending in 2004 delivered returns very much in line with the long-term average returns. But a market-timer who, unfortunately, missed the ten best days saw his returns drop by half, from 10.19% to only 5.10%. Missing the best twenty days caused the market timer to barely break even, seeing his returns drop to 1.26% per year. Market timers missing the best thirty days worth of gains lost an average of 2.04% per year, more than twelve percentage points less than the buy-and-hold investor realized.

Stock Selection: Wall Street Roulette

It should be clear from the discussion above, that attempting to ride stock market waves is a fool's errand for all but a select few. Accepting this fact is only Step One. Most investors, disabused by the notion that they can find success with an active strategy, will nevertheless assume that the secret to great returns is selecting the right stocks.

> If there are 10,000 people looking at the stocks and trying to pick winners, well, one in 10,000 is going to score, by chance alone, a great coup, and that's all that's going on. It's a game, it's a chance operation, and people think they are doing something purposeful…but they're really not.
>
> – Merton Miller, Nobel Laureate
> commenting for the PBS *Nova* special,
> *The Trillion Dollar Bet*

True believers in stock-picking will be dismayed to learn that research data clearly demonstrate that their odds are no better than their market timing counterparts. More than two hundred studies have been published that compare the performance of active investment managers with the market average. The results of these studies show that even with all the tools available to large professional managers, the vast majority underperform the market.

In general, the chances of a manager beating the market over a ten-year period were found to be 1-in-36 according to one study, 1-in-39 according to another, and only 1-in-41 in a third. By comparison, Las Vegas casinos offer better odds at 35-for-1 to those who correctly guess which number will come up on the next spin of the roulette wheel.

Mutual funds and pension funds are among the investment products that suffer from this underperformance. John C. Bogle, founder of the Vanguard mutual fund family and a strong proponent of low-cost index investment strategies, published a study entitled *Bogle on Equity Fund Selection.* He determined that just 2.5% (9 of 355) of actively managed stock mutual funds were able to beat the market over a thirty-year time frame. The odds, then, of choosing a winning mutual fund are about 1-in-39–slightly worse odds compared to playing roulette.

> There has always been a considerable number of pathetic dopes who busy themselves examining the last thousand numbers which have appeared on a roulette wheel, in search of a repeating pattern.
>
> – Fred Schwed, Jr., Author

The hypothetical buy-and-hold investor actually did very well compared to the performance of the typical mutual fund investor. Many individuals simply chase last year's winners and researchers found that they did not earn high returns. Although the funds they chose had good multi-year records, the average investor managed to earn only 3.7%, because he bought near the top and sold in frustration near the bottom. When compared to the more than 10% long-term average compounded rate of return generated by indexes, those funds–last year's winners–will be rightly deemed a waste of time. This startling finding has been documented in research by Lipper, a mutual fund rating service.

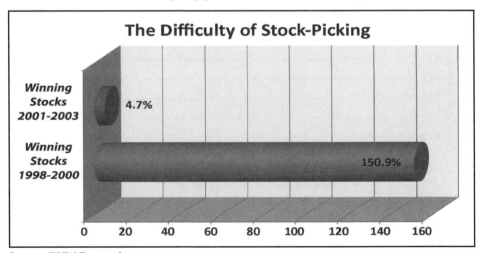

Source: RVW Research

Figure 2-2: Big winners in the stock market from 1998-2000 did not repeat their outstanding performance in the next three years.

Picking the best stocks for the future requires you to know today which companies will still be around ten years from now. The S&P 500® dates back only to 1957 (prior to that time it consisted of fewer stocks). Of the original five hundred companies, just seventy-four were still in existence thirty years later, but only twelve of those seventy-four delivered better performance than the Index itself. A mere 2.4% of the stocks were long-term winners, odds of about 1-in-42. The roulette wheel is looking even better! A stock-picker barely had 1-in-7 chance of picking a survivor.

And the odds are certainly stacked against your ability to pick a survivor that outperforms the market. You might have thought that GE would be a good stock to own, but it suffered through fifteen years of zero price appreciation beginning in 1965, and was devastated in the bear market of 2008. IBM and Gillette, both excellent companies, saw their stock prices decline by 65% during the 1960s and 1970s. These extended periods of decline and stagnation can cost you more than you realize–by owning a losing stock you are missing out on gains available elsewhere.

> We've long felt that the only value of stock forecasters is to make fortunetellers look good.
>
> – Warren Buffett

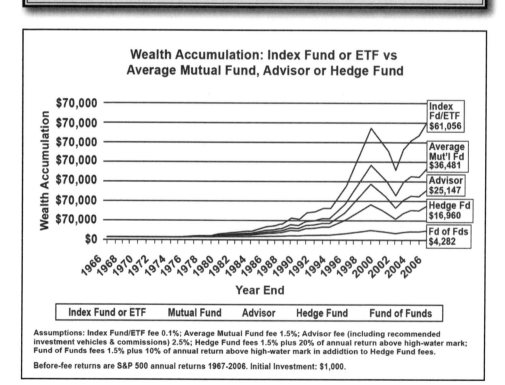

Wealth Accumulation: Index Fund or ETF vs Average Mutual Fund, Advisor or Hedge Fund

Assumptions: Index Fund/ETF fee 0.1%; Average Mutual Fund fee 1.5%; Advisor fee (including recommended investment vehicles & commissions) 2.5%; Hedge Fund fees 1.5% plus 20% of annual return above high-water mark; Fund of Funds fees 1.5% plus 10% of annual return above high-water mark in addidtion to Hedge Fund fees.

Before-fee returns are S&P 500 annual returns 1967-2006. Initial Investment: $1,000.

The good news is that you can always sell your losing stocks and have an opportunity to buy the next big winner, but since you missed the mark on the last one, chances are you'll buy a few more losers. That hope comes with a price. Active management means accumulating trading costs and paying commissions that may seem small but can add up quickly.

> The economists arrived at a devastating conclusion: it seemed just as plausible to attribute the success of top traders to sheer luck, rather than skill.
> – Transcript of the PBS *Nova* Special
> *The Trillion Dollar Bet*

When you do find a winner, eventually you'll want to take profits and reinvest them in something else destined for big returns. This is a good strategy, but you'll only get to keep part of the profits because of taxes. For investors living in states with high income tax rates, half of the profits could end up going to pay these tax bills.

No News Is Good News

Yet another challenge that stock-pickers face is determining the right time to go bargain hunting and buy stocks. To help with this, many turn to the media. Unfortunately, newspapers and magazines fare even worse than investment newsletter writers. *Business Week* famously proclaimed, "The Death of Equities." They asserted that inflation was destroying the stock market in 1979–three years later (to the day) a great bull market that would last eighteen years began. While anecdotal evidence is nice, and is usually what investors rely on, successful investing is actually a science, and we should require hard data before we believe anything. Believe it or not, the usefulness of magazine cover stories has undergone rigorous analysis.

The *Financial Analysts Journal* published a study by Thomas Arnold, John H. Earl, Jr., and David S. North, three finance professors at the University of Richmond. Their study, *Are Cover Stories Effective Contrarian Indicators?*, supports the idea that investors who rely on magazine covers for their investing advice are doomed to mediocre performance. The professors looked at how a company's stock performed after the company was featured in a cover story by one of the major weekly business publications–*BusinessWeek*, *Fortune*, and *Forbes*. They found that the magazines published favorable stories following periods of positive performance and negative stories following periods of subpar performance. Most significantly, they also showed that the appearance of a cover story tended to signal the end of the abnormal performance. Individuals who trade on such news, they concluded, were not likely to do well.

> I think the biggest myth about the stock market is that there are expert investors who can consistently beat the market. It just isn't true.
>
> – Burton G. Malkiel, Economist and Author
> *A Random Walk Down Wall Street*

But this phenomenon is not restricted to the stock market. At the height of the real estate bubble in late 2006, *Flipping Houses for Dummies* was published. This book promised that it would teach you how to "lay the foundation for successful flipping and bring home the bucks." Of course, by the time it hit the bookstores the housing market indexes had already peaked and were declining precipitously.

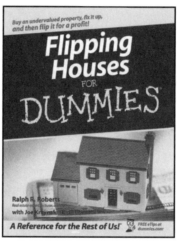

Figure 2-3: Proof that optimistic forecasting is not limited to the stock market.

Most investors would never think of steering their car down the highway using only their rear-view mirror, but that is often the best way to describe how they invest. They attempt to forecast, to predict the future, by looking at how others interpreted the recent past. The best thing to remember for your financial health is to avoid stock-pickers . . . who have no greater chance of beating the market than you have of beating the house at roulette. You also need to avoid market-timers and newspapers and magazines that sell more subscriptions with doom and gloom than with advice to buy and hold and sit tight through the corrections.

The solution is to always be in the market, and to always own the market. The best investment strategy is to simply own a well-diversified and global portfolio of index funds matched to your unique financial circumstances. Once you have constructed your portfolio, the hard work is over. Sit back, relax, and enjoy a nap!

> After spending many years in Wall Street and after making and losing millions of dollars I want to tell you this: It never was my thinking that made the big money for me. It always was my sitting. Got that? My sitting tight!
>
> – Jesse Livermore, Stock Trader (1877-1940)
> Known as *"The Great Bear of Wall Street"*

The Fallacy of Predictions and Prognostications

At the end of 2007, *BusinessWeek* continued its impressive string of failed stock and economic predictions when it published its annual Summary of Economic Forecasts for 2008. Every one of the fifty-four economists surveyed predicted that the US economy would not "sink into a recession." It would be, they all declared, a solid but unspectacular year. They weren't alone in failing to see what was coming.

Figure 2-4: *BusinessWeek's* famously bad market-timing call, "The Death of Equities," the cover story in its August 13, 1979 issue.

In July, 2009, a group of eminent British economists and constitutional experts wrote to the Queen bemoaning, "a failure of the collective imagination" that had led none of them to predict the credit crunch.

Philip Tetlock, an American psychologist, became so frustrated by the arrogance of punditry that he devised an unusual experiment. In 1984, Tetlock selected 284 academics, economists, and think-tankers–all were considered experts and made their livings predicting political and economic trends–and asked them for their predictions about how the future might turn out. Twenty years later, he revisited their predictions and the results were astounding. Most experts, Tetlock showed, are no better than "dart-throwing chimpanzees" at the prognostication game. Worse yet, when challenged about their mistakes, many of them failed to own up–some tried to fudge, while others claimed to have been right all along.

Part of the problem lies in the lack of accountability within the profession itself. Make a bold prediction and the journalists and TV cameras come running; no one remembers when it fails to come about. Paul Ehrlich's 1968 book, *Population Bomb*, for example, argued that the earth's population was growing far more quickly than our ability to feed it–and painted a terrifying picture of the era of mass starvation to come in the following decade . . . an era that utterly failed to materialize.

Chapter 3
Ten Reasons Why
Your Financial Advisor Is Not Your Friend

> The stockbroker services his clients in the same way that Bonnie and Clyde serviced banks.
>
> — William Bernstein, Author
> *The Four Pillars of Investing*

If you are like most people, you most likely look for the best in others. As such, you will probably take your investment advisor at face value. He surely is a fine fellow, completely ethical, and has impeccable morals. You may even be golf buddies or social friends. That being said, the nature of his business puts his interests directly at odds with yours.

He puts bread on his table by generating as large a collection of fees as possible. Every dollar he lines his pocket with is one dollar less in yours. He earns his greatest reward when he sells you the wrong mutual fund. Not only will he receive a fee for selling it to you, but he will make an additional fee after it loses money and, perhaps, when you buy a different one. The last thing he will ever tell you is to buy an index and hold it for twenty years, because it will significantly impair his bottom line.

There are few other things your broker conveniently may have "forgotten" to tell you.

- Unlike stocks, where commissions must be disclosed and most trades occur by "auction," you have no idea how much he will be making on your purchase of a bond. Those commissions are undisclosed because you buy from his inventory at his marked-up sales price. He buys low and sells high and earns additional profit on the "spread."

- Callable bonds are a "heads I win, tails you lose" proposition. If interest rates drop, higher-rate bonds will be redeemed and you will lose the interest payments you once counted on. On the other hand, if interest rates rise, you will be earning below-market rates, and losing purchasing power.

■ Tax-free municipal bonds may not be tax-free after all. If you're subject to the Alternative Minimum Tax, you're probably better off owning taxable corporate bonds.

■ Bond values are devastated by inflation: Between 1968 and 1982 the purchasing power of the US dollar dropped by half. When redeemed, the principal will not be enough to buy what it once might have ten, twenty, or thirty years earlier.

■ Although the US stock markets have historically delivered total returns of about 11% annually, the average investor has managed to obtain just 2.6%. They buy high and sell low—tending to buy what's in vogue rather than what is durable. Such actions are prescriptions for disaster.

■ You'll never know what you're really paying for asset management; there are so many layers of fees, costs, and expenses in a typical broker's "wrap account" that the total costs are carefully hidden from view. Some mutual funds have internal expenses that rob investors of 4% or more of their annual returns . . . many actively managed mutual funds report expense ratios of 2% or more. Mutual funds may also generate taxable "phantom income" for which you will receive an IRS Form 1099 reflecting income you neither earned nor received.

■ Investing is a science, not an art.

> Investing should be like watching paint dry or watching grass grow. If you want excitement, take $800 and go to Las Vegas.
> – Paul Samuelson, Nobel Laureate

If you still believe your investment advisor is your friend, you may need to read what Harvard economist Michael Jensen wrote in 1976–in one of the most widely cited papers on economics in the last thirty-five years: "Theory of the firm: Managerial behavior, agency costs and ownership structure"– arguing that the interests of most fund managers are significantly different from their shareholders, and try to recall whether your advisor has ever discussed any of the following issues with you.

1. *Your investment advisor does not have to act in your best interest.*

Brokers, in particular, are exempt from many rules that require other investment advisors to place the client ahead of their own interests. But most brokers and investment advisors have interests of their own and these interests are all too often in conflict with the goals of their clients.

2. *There are more costs associated with a mutual fund than you know about.*

> It is difficult to systemically beat the market. But it is not difficult to systemically throw money down a rat hole by generating commissions (and other costs). Investment managers sell for the price of a Picasso what routinely turns out to be paint-by-number art.
>
> – Patricia C. Dunn, former Vice Chairman
> Barclays Global Investors

Ms. Dunn probably knows what she is talking about. Barclays Global Investors is one of the world's leading money management firms. Mutual funds are often sold with a sales charge, known as a *load*. Buying or selling a stock always involves a commission. Those charges are easy to see. Less obvious are the annual fees paid to the fund manager and the costs of all those trades they make in the fund's portfolio as they pursue profits on your behalf. Even harder to see, until the end of the year, are the costs associated with taxes. Although disclosed, none of these layers of expenses are easily explained in the prospectuses that investment advisors hand out.

Altogether, these expenses can add up to 25% of the total possible returns from stock market gains. What could have been a 10% annual rate of return can be reduced to 7.5% just as a result of the *internal expenses* associated with owning an otherwise top-performing, actively managed mutual fund. Given the difficulty of identifying the best performers in advance–in a universe of more than 10,000 funds–you are likely to see even worse returns. Internal expenses and an inability to always invest in the biggest winners cause most investors to significantly underperform the market.

3. *Sales commissions can cost much more than you may realize.*

When an investment advisor recommends a fund to a client, that fund will usually be a load fund, and the load is pocketed by the broker (or other middlemen) as payment for providing the service of helping you pick a good fund. These loads range from a few percent of your initial investment to as much as 8.5% of your hard-earned nest egg.

The first thing your investment advisor should be required to tell you is that there is no real difference historically between the load funds and no-load funds in terms of performance. True no-load funds allow you to invest directly without paying any upfront sales charges to the fund or an investment advisor. In fact, Morningstar, Inc., a leading provider of independent investment research, concluded in a recent study that even when the negative effect of the load is excluded from a fund's performance evaluation, no-load funds actually had a superior record compared to load funds over three- and five-year periods ending in 2006. In short, funds that don't impose any fees or sales loads to purchase them have, repeatedly, outperformed those that investment advisors charge you to find.

> Wall Street is the only place where people ride to work in a Rolls Royce to get advice from those who take the subway.
> – Warren Buffett

A simple example quantifies that study. As a result of compounding, the initial sales charges lower your returns for as long as you own a mutual fund. This is because the dollars you paid the investment advisor could have been working for you instead of for him. If you were to own a fund for fifteen years, a 6% sales charge will have the effect of lowering your total return by 0.5% a year.

Many investors access equities through "tax-deferred" variable annuity products, where agents earn high commissions, extra layers of internal expenses are often very costly, and there are additional fees to liquidate prematurely known as *surrender charges*.

4. Annual fees come off the top.

Mutual fund returns are net of charges and costs for management, marketing, and other administrative expenses. Most investors never see the total because the layers of fees are detailed in the fine print of the prospectus and annual reports. If you read these documents, and most investors do not, you'll soon realize that all these fees conspire to lower your returns and can sometimes total 3% or more annually. Compounded over many years, this is a significant amount to pay considering that most managers underperform the market.

Marketing fees seem like price gouging. More formally known as *distribution* or *"12b-1" fees*, these are charged to shareholder accounts to cover "distribution expenses" and may also be used to fund shareholder services. The "12b-1 fees" get their name from the SEC rule that authorizes a fund to pay them as an expense of the fund. Distribution expenses include such things as the cost of advertising and selling fund shares, compensating brokers and investment advisors who sell fund shares, paying for the printing and mailing of prospectuses to current and prospective investors, and the printing and mailing of sales literature. Regulators limit a fund's 12b-1 "management" fee to a maximum of 0.75% a year, but that fee is assessed quarterly, which can skew the equation in favor of the fund. Also permitted is an additional 0.25% 12b-1 "distribution" fee.

> Active management means that the compounding costs of fees and taxes largely offset your compounding portfolio growth.
> – Rip Van Winkle Wisdom

Mutual funds may be the only business model where current customers are explicitly charged advertising expenses. Most other businesses would budget for this expense, use the dollars wisely, and factor it into the retail price of their products or services–simply a part of the overall cost of doing business. With mutual funds, however, the board of directors can spend more as the fund's assets grow, and the advertising agencies know this so they meet the needs of the client and create more advertising campaigns.

No published studies have shown that larger funds outperform smaller funds and, in fact, it often becomes harder for active managers to follow their disciplined approach as fund assets grow and new money pours in. This means marketing and distribution fees may actually hurt future fund performance, while at the same time diminishing your current returns.

5. *Little, if any, training is required to become an investment advisor.*

Offering financial advice has become a growth industry in recent years. To serve the public, all you have to do is pass an exam to sell life insurance and pass a couple of tests about the securities industry but only about 40%-50% of all FINRA (Financial Industry Regulatory Authority) first-time examinees pass. Alternately, you may elect to become a Registered Investment Advisor and take a relatively easy Series 65 exam. After passing the exams and being approved by FINRA and the state regulators, new associates in a firm might receive additional sales training, but few firms offer real training on investments or financial planning.

The newly minted investment advisor is usually given a sales manual and a commission sheet. He frequently tries to sell you investment or insurance products without fully appreciating the tax implications for your particular situation, the impact on your retirement income, or any potential estate-planning ramifications. Instead of understanding your specific financial requirements and circumstances, he offers a "canned" sales pitch that you could just as easily hear on a used car lot. A new associate is more likely to be told to contact everyone he knows–their "warm market"–than to call on folks they don't ("cold calling"). This is your financial partner.

> **6. Certain investments or insurance products pay the advisor more than other investments.**

Mutual fund families often employ salesmen, known as *internal wholesalers*, to promote their funds to the salesmen who will sell it to you. These layers of salesmen can be expensive, so they need to deliver results. As many companies know, one of the best ways to boost sales is to boost commissions or offer incentives to the sales force. This ultimately leads to higher prices for the end consumer, an inferior product, or both. In the investment business, the most appropriate product for the client, such as low-cost index funds, ends up paying the lowest commission to the advisor.

7. *Mutual funds shares are sold in "classes" – A, B, and C – and all three are bad for you.*

The various fee structures confuse investors, making it easier for investment advisors and fund managers to make more money. Class A shares charge a front-end load, reducing the net amount you invest in the fund. A 5% load means that only $9,500 of every $10,000 investment goes to work for you. The funds usually charge a 12b-1 fee, but it's limited to a maximum of 0.25%. "Breakpoints," which are simply volume discounts, reduce the amount of the sales load. The first breakpoint for many load funds usually occurs when an account holder has at least $50,000 invested. Loads continue to drop at various breakpoints (such as $100,000, $250,000, and $500,000) until they disappear entirely, typically at $1,000,000.

Class B shares don't charge a front-end load, and they often impose a higher 12b-1 management fee, typically the maximum 0.75%. However, the shares frequently carry a "back-end load," called a *contingent deferred sales charge* (CDSC), which investors pay if they redeem their shares too soon after purchase. The CDSC gradually declines over five to seven years, when it is eliminated. Another year or two later, Class B shares convert to Class A shares, and the 12b-1 fee is reduced. Mutual fund companies and investment advisors claim that the deferred sales charge encourages long-term holding by imposing a penalty to sell early. That's a small carrot which often dangles from a very big stick for some investors. Occasionally, Class B shares are misrepresented by sales reps as "no-load" mutual fund shares.

Class C shares typically charge the maximum permissible 12b-1 fees, a total of 1%, and they carry a small CDSC of 1% or 2%, usually only for the first year after you buy the shares. Class C shares do not convert to Class A shares, and the 12b-1 fee remains high the entire time you own the fund.

All this is confusing to most investors, and this is how some investment advisors profit. When they sell a Class A share, they receive only the front-end load. When an investment advisor sells a Class B share, there is no front-end load, so the distributor uses its own money and pays a commission. Because of the potential for investment advisors to make more money selling Class B shares to large clients (when it's not in the client's best interest), and to avoid problems with the regulators, funds no longer permit the purchase of Class B shares when the amount invested would qualify for a breakpoint. Failing to advise a client of an available breakpoint is a sales violation.

8. Wrap accounts pile fee upon fee in a single account.

A popular investment account sold by investment advisors is known as a *wrap account*, in which all account expenses are bundled into a single (flat or fixed) fee. Charges of 1%–3% of the account's assets are deducted from the balance at regular intervals to pay for all trading, administrative, research, and advisory expenses. And you may eventually discover layers of undisclosed fees that also negatively affect your account.

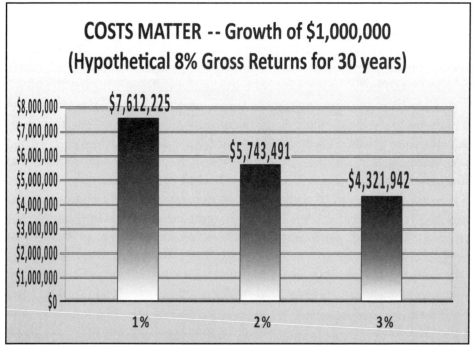

Figure 3-1: The diminishing effect of mutual fund sales charges and annual investment expenses or advisory "wrap" fees on long-term portfolio value cannot be ignored.

Investment advisors sell these accounts claiming that one advantage to a wrap account is that it protects investors from over-trading, or *churning*, since the advisor does not receive a commission. Excessive trading in an customer's account to generate extra commissions can happen, so the theory is not without merit. Because the wrap account is charged a flat annual fee, the most you can be charged is the fixed percentage.

With mutual funds, which are often held in wrap accounts, you might actually be charged twice. The mutual fund manager still charges his full fee inside the fund, and that internal expense drags down your potential annual returns. Half of the stock market's average gains could be lost to the combination of a fund's internal expenses and the external investment advisor's annual fee. You experience both the internal and external investment advisors' fees whether the market is up or down.

Finally, the SEC realized that wrap accounts did not help investors and took action to stop this industry abuse. In late 2007, they ordered brokers and advisors to stop offering these accounts. The industry responded with prompt compliance, and converted many client wrap accounts into another type of account known as *fee-based, nondiscretionary advisory accounts*. In these accounts, you can hold virtually any combination of individual stocks, bonds, exchange-traded funds, mutual funds, and cash investments. Investment advisors may offer comprehensive advice, but the investor controls the final decisions since the advisor must get the client's permission before making changes to investments. Fees are still assessed as a percentage of assets in your account, so not much has really changed.

> Your stockbroker earns money from you, not for you.
> – Rip Van Winkle Wisdom

What your advisor might not tell you is that although the fee-based, nondiscretionary advisory account is legal, it continues to look exactly like the old, illegal wrap account. There are still multiple layers of fees, other costs within the underlying funds, and fees paid to the fund's investment manager. These accounts provide an opportunity for the investment advisor to portray the costs more attractively, positioning himself, the salesman, as an "objective" judge of value. By effectively moving to the other side of the table, alongside the investor, the "Investment Advisor" (not "stockbroker") secures a large regular income and positions himself to retain you and, more importantly, your assets, even if a particular fund manager underperforms.

You *thought* you heard the advisor say, "If you don't make money, I don't make money," but what he really meant was, "If you don't make money, I still make money . . . just not as much."

The fact remains that the advisor's fee is charged based on net (or average) assets under management. The account value may be lower than last year, the fee may be lower than last year, but the advisor still gets his fee. He has the ability to make money even when you're losing yours.

9. There is no evidence that "house funds" are a good investment.

"House funds" are run by the major Wall Street brokerage firms. It seems logical that Wall Street powerhouses would have the best information on which to base investment decisions, and you would expect their funds to be among the top performers year after year. Studies reveal, however, no evidence exists to prove that such funds do any better than independently managed funds. Actually, most house funds fare worse than independently managed funds.

Then why do brokers sell them? House funds pay higher commissions than other funds. House funds create great opportunities for conflict of interest, encouraging brokers to act in their own best interest and not yours by willingly putting you into a subpar performer, when commissions and other incentives are the broker's only real justification.

To many who work in the investment advice field, the most important aspect of the job is to make sales. Although a small number actually work for hourly compensation alone, most stockbrokers are paid according to their sales activity. From their perspective, hyperactive trading is the best thing they can offer. That way, they get paid when you buy *and* when you sell, and the cycle never ends for the lucky broker.

In addition to the fact that it is in their best interest to sell you something, brokers have even less requirement to work on your behalf than investment advisors. While investment advisors are under a "fiduciary responsibility" mandate, stockbrokers and registered representatives are merely bound by the "Prudent Man Rule," which has been adopted in every state. Barring only criminal intent, this rule requires that a person must:

> observe how men of prudence, discretion and intelligence manage their own affairs, not in regard to speculation, but in regard to the permanent disposition of their funds, considering the probable income, as well as the probable safety of the capital to be invested. If that person's advice would seem reasonable to a "prudent" man, then nothing wrong has happened if someone else suffers a loss as the result of following that advice. [*Harvard College v. Armory*, 9 Pick (26 Mass) 446, 461 (1830)]

While you would probably never consider seeing a doctor who operated under a philosophy such as the Prudent Man Rule, this concept dominates the legal environment of the brokerage industry.

10. You can't sue your broker for his bad advice; you have to submit to mandatory, binding arbitration.

All investors agree to this when they open a brokerage account. The advantage, according to your broker, is that you won't ever have to go to court to settle disputes; you'll use a system run by FINRA, which was created in the 2007 merger of the two largest "self-regulatory organizations" (SROs), the National Association of Securities Dealers (NASD) and the New York Stock Exchange (NYSE).

All disputes are heard by a panel of three persons knowledgeable about the securities industry (they may be "public" or "nonpublic" persons–a nonpublic person has worked inside the industry). While you will get a fair hearing, the fact that the arbitration panel knows the rules far better than the average investor usually means that you will lose in this setting.

A study conducted by securities lawyer Daniel Solin and Edward O'Neal, a former finance professor, shows that the arbitration win rate, meaning that investors win "damages" from brokers, was only 44% in 2004. [According to the FINRA Dispute Resolution website, that number was 45% for arbitrations in 2009, however, the total percentage of claims that resulted in some form of monetary recovery was actually 70%, including regulatory recoveries outside arbitration.]

The research was difficult to conduct. The researchers actually had to sue the NASD to obtain permission to study the awards. In the end, they obtained 14,000 NASD and NYSE arbitration records from 1995 through 2004. They found that the larger the claim, the smaller the recovery. For those with claims exceeding $250,000, only 12% of investors were successful. When complaints involving mutual funds are not at the top of the list, they are second only to complaints involving individual stocks.

What conclusion can be drawn from this? If you are among the lucky few whose investment advisor has encouraged you to buy and hold index funds, then you are probably sleeping easily knowing that he has given you sound advice. On the other hand, if your advisor convinced you to invest in actively managed funds or a wrap account arrangement and has failed to discuss with you the points enumerated above, you may want to reconsider on whose side he really is.

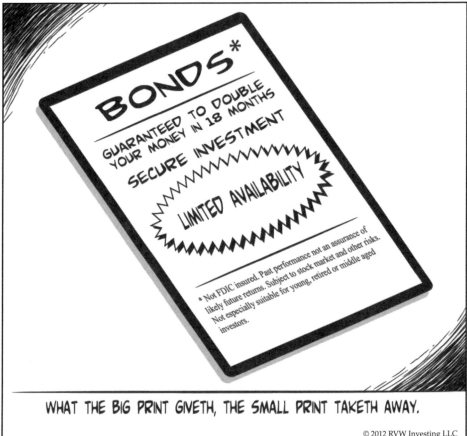

WHAT THE BIG PRINT GIVETH, THE SMALL PRINT TAKETH AWAY.

Chapter 4
Debunking the Myth:
How to Beat at Least 80%
of All Active Managers with Index Funds

> All the time and effort people devote to picking the right fund, the hot hand, or the great manager have, in most cases, led to no advantage.
> – Peter Lynch, Author
> *Beating the Street*

It has been a matter of consensus for some time that the vast majority of active managers underperform the market. Nevertheless, investors continue to fund their failed attempts. Why earn submarket returns in order to pay these managers' fees when you could just own the market? Statistically speaking, you will beat at least 80% of these active managers simply by owning index funds.

The Origins of Index Funds

In 1975, John Bogle, founder of the Vanguard Group, presented a radical, landscape-reshaping idea to his board of directors. A year into the life of the firm, Bogle had his mind set on the creation of a new breed of low-cost mutual funds. Instead of relying on active stock-picking and market-timing, his new fund would attempt to duplicate the performance of the index by buying each of the Standard & Poor's 500® Index's 500 stocks. The goal was to match, as closely as possible, the market's performance as measured by the S&P, and he believed it could be accomplished by allocating the fund's assets to the component stocks of the Index itself.

In his own account of the inception of index funds, Bogle writes:

I projected the costs of managing an index fund to be 0.3% per year in operating expenses and 0.2% per year in transaction costs. Since fund annual costs at that time appeared to be about 2.0%, I concluded that an index fund should reasonably be expected to provide an annual return of 1.5% above a managed fund.

By simply lowering expenses, Bogle believed it should be possible to outperform the market. Time has proven his thesis to be deadly accurate . . . beyond even his own expectations.

> The miracle of compounding returns is overwhelmed by the tyranny of compounding costs.
>
> – John C. Bogle, Founder
> Vanguard Group

In the real world, the gap between the performance of the market and the performance of actively managed mutual funds has actually been significantly wider than the 1.5% theorized by Bogle in 1975. During the 1990s, the total shortfall between actively managed mutual funds and the market, as measured by the S&P 500®, was surprisingly much larger–more than double, in fact, at 3.4% per year.

The difference between actively managed funds and passively managed index funds is very easily explained. Bogle attributes the difference to four factors: (1) expenses, (2) turnover, (3) sector, and (4) cash reserves–each of which is discussed below.

1. **Expenses**. The expense ratio of the average fund, the amount that a fund charges its shareholders to manage their money every year, was about 1.3% during the 1990s. In a trend that demonstrates corporate greed, average mutual fund fees have been increasing over time. By comparison, the Vanguard S&P 500 fund's expense ratio is 0.19%.

Over twenty five years, these costs add up. A $10,000 investment in an index mutual fund made in 1980 would have returned an average 12.5% a year and grown to $170,800 by 2005. In the same period, the average actively managed mutual fund delivered a respectable 10% a year, but $10,000 would have grown to just $98,200. Costs of only 2.5% a year, however, reduce profits by a whopping 57% over the long term!

2. **Turnover**. In pursuit of market-beating returns, active managers tend to buy and sell their holdings at a rapid pace. There is no time to give a stock a chance to show that it is a long-term winner because active managers are measured on short-term performance. Marketing departments care

about what happened last month, last quarter, or maybe last year. The natural consequence of this pressure to perform results in investors missing out on long-term gains. Also, the transaction costs of constantly buying and selling so many shares consumes an additional 0.7% of return every year.

On the bright side, portfolio turnover in an index fund is typically 5% or lower. This means that buying and selling may cost shareholders less than 0.1%. The difference of 0.6% a year increases the wealth of the investor rather than those employed at trading desks at mutual fund firms.

> I think investors have to have a little less self-confidence and realize, to put it in a very harsh way, that the mutual fund industry in particular is not only an industry where you don't get what you pay for, it turns out, examine the data, you get precisely what you don't pay for.
>
> And therefore, if you pay nothing, you get everything. You get the market's return if you don't pay anything to get it. So the index fund is giving you the market return less a tenth of 1%, and that has to be the answer. And I feel a little guilty talking about index funds because I did create that first one all those years ago . . . .
>
> –John C. Bogle to Steve Forbes,
> *Forbes*, January 2009

During the 1990s, the S&P 500® outperformed not only the average diversified mutual fund and active manager, but delivered returns that were better than the rest of the market. The performance of the entire stock market can be measured by an index known as the Wilshire 5000 Total Market Index, which tracks more than 98% of the stocks that are traded. The return for the Wilshire 5000 was a full percentage point lower than the S&P 500® for that decade. It was better to own the S&P 500® Index instead of the average stock.

3. **Sector.** Since active managers are looking for winning stocks, they are buying and selling these average stocks in a futile pursuit of higher gains. They need to hold so many stocks that they tend to make the same mistake individual investors make and chase yesterday's winners. They end up making market-lagging bets in the sectors of the economy that did well last quarter. These sector bets hold down returns and

partly explain why active management usually fails to beat index funds.

4. **Cash Reserves.** The fourth factor that hurts actively managed funds is cash reserves. Managers must hold cash reserves in order to meet anticipated shareholder redemption requests, and the manager also chooses to hold cash because he tries to time the market. Holding part of his clients' portfolios as cash reserves can be a very expensive practice if the market moves higher. This active decision made by fund managers explains a significant part of the underperformance between mutual funds and the market.

Other mutual fund management companies noticed the success that Bogle and Vanguard Group's low-cost index funds enjoyed and began responding with offerings of their own. There are now funds to match mid-cap indexes, small-cap indexes, small-cap growth indexes, small-cap value indexes, foreign indexes, as well as variations on all of these and many other indexes. Each of these other index funds, in all probability, will also outperform most managed funds.

> Most of the mutual fund investments I have are index funds.
> – Charles Schwab, Author
> *Guide to Financial Independence*

While Bogle correctly identified the likely causes of the underperformance of actively managed mutual funds, most investors still believe, or, perhaps, more accurately hope, that they can identify the long-term winners from the thousands of available investment options. It might be possible to spot tomorrow's best performers by answering a few questions:

1. **Does the manager really have the skills needed to beat the market, or was recent performance just a run of good luck?**

2. **If the recent performance came about because of a unique skill, will that actually be the right skill to continue delivering outperformance in the future? Or, was the skill only useful in the most recent market?**

3. **How much time do you need to decide whether a manager has proven that he has the necessary skills to consistently outperform the market in coming decades?**

Answer to Question 1

Most researchers agree that stock prices are affected by newsworthy events, which tend to be unpredictable. This, in turn, means that stock movement is also unpredictable. Therefore, one skill required to consistently beat the market is the ability to predict random events. This is not entirely impossible. Successful investors such as Warren Buffett and George Soros have demonstrated an uncanny ability to understand the impact of news on stocks over the long run, and they have profitted from their insights. However, investors like these are more likely to be the exceptions to the rule rather than the models the average fund manager can emulate.

Another problem that active managers face is that when news happens, it is almost immediately priced into the market. Usually within minutes, traders have assessed the impact of the event on a stock and bought or sold in sufficient quantity to bring the price back to equilibrium. While it would be challenging to know the news in advance, that is not enough to deliver consistent profits. Successful managers would also need to predict the impact of the news on the price of the stock. It is fairly common for a company to report good earnings and see its shares fall because the earnings were less than the optimistic estimates that analysts were looking for. These events, and the market's reactions, defy prediction.

This leads us to conclude that more often than not, the answer to the first of our three questions is: *No.* While a few individuals have the skills needed to outperform the market, the odds of finding a successful active manager early enough in the process to enjoy the large gains are against you.

Answer to Question 2

Turning to the second question, there are periods of time when an active manager can do no wrong. Reviewing three- or five-year periods of mutual fund returns, we can always spot managers who have enjoyed consistent gains. A study was done that sorted manager performance over various three- and five-year periods. The best managers in one period occasionally delivered good results in the next period, but the rankings showed that performance between subsequent periods was entirely random. The best manager in one time frame could be the best in the next, or in the middle, or near the bottom. Researchers were unable to find any solid correlation between past performance and future performance.

It does seem that some managers are able to pick stocks well in a bull market, while others invest profitably during a bear market. However, since it is nearly impossible to predict whether stocks will be moving higher or lower in the months ahead, these managers are likely to give back their gains as market conditions switch. These observations lead us to conclude that the answer to our second question is, generally speaking, *No.*

> I realized technical stock analysis didn't work when I turned the charts upside down and didn't get a different answer.
> – Warren Buffett

Answer to Question 3

Studies indicate that stocks consistently deliver positive returns that beat inflation over any twenty-year period. The same cannot be said of fund managers. Few remain in the business for twenty years, and those that do generally show a great deal of variance in their returns from year to year. It seems unlikely that we can quantitatively identify tomorrow's investment superstars.

The fact that actively managed mutual funds underperform the broad market has been well known for a long time. Probably the first to document this was Michael C. Jensen, in his 1967 article, "The Performance of Mutual Funds in the Period 1945-1964," which appeared in the *Journal of Finance* [23:2, 389–416]. Jensen's results shocked the investment community by showing that if investors had held a broad-based portfolio of common stocks at the same risk level as mutual funds, they would have earned 15% more than the average fund. He demonstrated that nearly a quarter of all funds outperformed the market but had taken on greater risk to do so.

Other studies have reached similar conclusions. An inherent problem in studying fund performances over the long term is that the funds rarely survive long enough to provide the necessary data. Commenting on the results of his study which revealed that about two-thirds of funds failed over a twenty-five-year period, Bogle says, "There are many reasons that funds disappear, few of them good." The answer to our final question is, simply: *You cannot afford to take **that** much time!*

Of the funds that remain long enough to acquire decades of performance data, few distinguish themselves. Although results vary by study, generally only 5%–10% of surviving funds outperform the market by more than 2% per year. The reality is that only one or two out of a hundred funds which existed at the beginning of any study both survived *and* outperformed the market.

> You know the stories: "The Top Ten Mutual Funds to Buy Now," "How to Double Your Money This Year," personality profiles that read like fan magazines. Stock touting pieces that praise any path to profits. We've all done these stories, in one form or another. It's investment pornography.
>
>   – Jane Bryant Quinn, Financial Writer
>   *Newsweek* Contributor

The challenge of picking a long-term winner is even more daunting than the numbers might allow. Widely regarded as one of the world's greatest investors, Warren Buffett noted that "a fat wallet is the enemy of superior returns." This means it's easier to beat the market with a small mutual fund than it is with one which has a large amount of assets under management. Numerous studies confirm Buffett's observation.

> The rear-view mirror is one thing; the windshield is another.
>   – Warren Buffett

Once considered the best mutual fund of its time, Fidelity Magellan has been stuck in the doldrums for decades. Magellan, which helped popularize mutual funds and the virtues of active management by delivering 29% annualized compounding returns from 1977 to 1990 under stellar stock-picker Peter Lynch, has been hemorrhaging money. One of the first funds to earn Morningstar's coveted *Five Star* rating when that system of evaluation was first introduced, Magellan's assets have now plunged from a height of over $110 billion to around $23 billion. Four of those five stars have been lost, and it has trailed 95% of comparable funds for the three years ending March 2011.

Agreeing with Buffett, Bogle's research demonstrated that among the few funds that outperformed the market over the long term, most of them achieved their best returns before they had a large amount of assets under management. He noticed that they, too, tended to underperform after the public learned of their success and began pouring money into the funds. Sudden large inflows create pressure to deploy funds that effectively undermined the manager's performance. Bogle concluded that funds with short-term success are doomed to subpar performance in the future as their increasing size limits the manager's investment options.

> It would be satisfying to settle the debate one of these days with a headline reading "Active Management Triumphs over Passive" or "Passive Management Vanquishes Active Approach."
>
> – Tom Stabile, Writer
> *Financial Times*

Bogle offers a corollary to the fact that more than 80% of active fund managers will fail to beat the market: *"Don't look for the needle in the haystack. Just buy the haystack."*

In other words, stop worrying about trying to guess which fund manager will have the best twenty-five-year record twenty-five years from now; buy an index fund and enjoy the full returns that the market offers.

Chapter 5
Indexes Unveiled

> A rising tide lifts all boats, but every year some vessels in the stock market spring a leak. Broad diversification ensures they won't sink the whole portfolio.
>
> – Weston Wellington, Vice President
> Dimensional Fund Advisors

In polite conversation, people know how to appropriately avoid conversations about religion and politics. That leaves many with only a few topics of discussion, such as sports or the arts. The one topic bandied about most, however, might very well be the stock market. *The Dow was up a hundred points . . . NASDAQ was down twenty points . . . the S&P 500® was flat.* To the uninitiated, it is not clear at all to what these oblique monikers are referring. Generally, when people talk about the "market" behaving in a certain way, they are referring to indexes. --

A stock market index is a basket of stocks whose price reflects the combined value of its components. The stocks that make up an index often share some common feature such as the fact that they all trade on the same stock market exchange, they all belong to the same industry, or they all have similar market capitalizations. Many indexes are maintained by news organizations, such as the Dow Jones Averages, other service firms, like the S&P 500®, or financial services firms like Morgan Stanley. Indexes are commonly used to as benchmarks against which to measure the performance of portfolios such as mutual funds.

Stock market indexes may be classified in many ways. The broadest-based indexes represent the performance of the entire stock market. The most common indexes are broad-based and include the stocks of large companies listed on a nation's largest stock exchanges, such as the Dow Jones Industrial Average and S&P 500® Index. Similar indexes provide measures of market activity in other countries. Examples include the FTSE 100 in Britain, the CAC 40 in France, the DAX in Germany, the Nikkei 225 in Japan, the Sensex in India, and the Hang Seng Index in Hong Kong.

Specialized indexes have also been created to track the performance of specific sectors of the market. The grandfather of all indexes, the Dow Jones Transportation Average, for example, consists of twenty companies in the transportation industry, including railroads and trucking businesses. Other indexes track companies with even more specialized criteria. The American Stock Exchange Interactive Week Internet Index tracks stocks of forty-two companies that sell products and services related to the Internet.

The Dow Jones Industrial Average (also referred to as the DJIA, Dow 30, or, informally, the Dow Jones, or simply, "the Dow") is one of several stock market indexes created in the late 1800s by *Wall Street Journal* editor, and Dow Jones & Company co-founder, Charles Dow. Dow compiled the index as a way to gauge the industrial performance of the US economy. It is the second oldest continuous US market index after the Dow Jones Transportation Average.

> In the long run the stock market indexes fluctuate around the long-term upward trend of earnings per share.
> – Sir John Templeton

Today, the Dow average consists of thirty of the largest and most widely held public companies in the US The "industrial" portion of the name is, for the most part, historical, because most of the thirty companies have nothing to do with heavy industry today. The "average" is price-weighted, meaning we should be able to add up the prices of the thirty stocks, divide by thirty, and obtain the average price. However, over the years, there have been a large number of stock splits and other "technical" adjustments to the average which have changed the way the average is calculated today. Each time a component stock has a split or issues a stock dividend, the value by which the sum of all prices is divided to generate the value of the index, the "divisor," changes to reflect the change in number of outstanding shares. As of September 2011, the DJIA divisor was 0.132129493. Because the divisor is less than one, the value of the index is higher than the sum of the component stock prices ($1/0.132129493 = 7.568333$).

The DJIA, when first published on May 26, 1896, represented the average of twelve stocks from key American industries. Of those original twelve, only General Electric is currently part of the average.

In a vibrant and dynamic economy, there are clearly no longer "evergreen" companies. Indexing allows an investor to be sure he is participating in the ongoing evolution of the economy. New companies that come into being will automatically be included in the portfolio, while enterprises that no longer exist will be dropped. So while holding an index is passive from the standpoint of the investor, the portfolio itself is internally dynamic and changing in response to the changes in the economy.

When it was first published, the Dow Jones Industrial Average stood at 40.94. It was computed as a direct average by simply adding the individual stock prices of its components and dividing by twelve, the number of stocks in the index.

The number of stocks in the index was increased to twenty in 1916, and to thirty in 1928. Components change irregularly at the discretion of the Dow Jones Company. The components have been changed forty-eight times since 1896, the last such change occurring on June 8, 2009, when Travelers Companies and Cisco Systems, Inc. replaced Citigroup Incorporated and General Motors Corporation, respectively.

Milestones in the History of
the Dow Jones Industrial Average
(100 on January 12, 1906)

MILESTONE	FIRST RECORDED	DAYS TO REACH
1,000	NOV 14, 1972	27,930
2,000	JAN 8, 1987	5,168
3,000	APR 17, 1991	1,560
4,000	FEB 23, 1995	1,408
5,000	NOV 21, 1995	271
6,000	OCT 14, 1996	328
7,000	FEB 13, 1997	122
8,000	JUL 16, 1997	153
9,000	APR 6, 1998	264
10,000	MAR 29, 1999	357
11,000	MAY 3, 1999	35
12,000	OCT 19, 2006	2,726
13,000	APR 25, 2007	188
14,000	JUL 19, 2007	85

Source: Dow Jones & Company and RVW Research

Table 5-1: The time between major milestones in the Dow varies a great deal, highlighting the risk of being out of the market and missing a significant gain.

Movement in the Dow has been steadily upward, mirroring the strong growth of the US economy. Although it took more than seventy-six years for the Dow to reach its first 1,000 milestone, the Average surpassed

14,000 in less than thirty-five years. All of the Dow's "1,000" milestones are highlighted below. The DJIA has never closed lower than 28.48 (August 8, 1896) and reached an all-time closing high of 14,164.53 on October 9, 2007.

The S&P 500® is an index based on the stocks of five hundred large-cap companies, most of which are American. The index is the most widely known of the many indexes owned and maintained by Standard & Poor's, a division of information services powerhouse McGraw-Hill. The S&P 500® index forms part of the broader S&P 1500®, measuring the performance of the US stock market, and the S&P Global 1200® stock market index, which is designed to reflect worldwide trading activity.

> The fundamental impulse that sets and keeps the capitalist engine in motion comes from the new consumers, goods, the new methods of production . . . that incessantly revolutionizes the economic structure from within . . . destroying the old one . . . creating a new one. This process of Creative Destruction is the essential fact about capitalism.
> – Joseph Schumpeter, Economist
> *Capitalism, Socialism and Democracy 1942*

All of the stocks in the S&P 500® are large, publicly held companies and trade on one of the two largest US stock markets, the New York Stock Exchange and the NASDAQ. After the Dow Jones Industrial Average, the S&P 500® is the most widely watched index of US stocks. It is a component of the "Leading Economic Index" maintained by *The Conference Board*, a non-governmental organization that monitors the ten key variables comprising its Index.

Many index funds and exchange-traded funds track the performance of the S&P 500® by holding the same stocks as the index, in the same proportions, thereby attempting to match its performance. Partly because of this, a company which has its stock added to the index may see a quick jump in its stock price as the managers of the mutual funds must purchase that company's stock in order to match the funds' composition to that of the S&P 500® index. Likewise, a company removed from the index may experience a sudden decline in its stock price.

The S&P 500® index is often used as a benchmark in stock and mutual fund performance charts for comparison. Charts usually show the S&P 500® index with the performance of the target stock or fund overlaid. Managers seek to outperform the index, otherwise they would add no value to the investment process.

The first S&P stock market index consisted of ninety companies and was called the S&P 90. It was introduced in 1923 and was published on a daily basis; no intraday quotes were available for the index at that time. A larger index of 423 companies was also published weekly. On March 4, 1957, the broader, real-time stock market index of 500 stocks was introduced. This was made possible by advancements in computer technology that allowed the index to be calculated and distributed in real time. Although the S&P 500® Index was created in 1957, it has since been extrapolated back in time, making data for the series available since 1923. The average time a company spends being part of the S&P 500® index has dropped from seventy-five years in 1937 to fifteen years today.

The S&P 500® includes both "growth" stocks, and generally less volatile "value" stocks; it also includes stocks from both the NASDAQ stock market and the NYSE. Assorted sub-indexes are now available to track only the growth or value components of this and many other indexes.

> Stock certificates are deeds of ownership in business enterprises and not betting slips.
>
> – J. Paul Getty, Industrialist

Growth stocks are shares of companies whose earnings are anticipated to increase at a rate faster than the broader market. Because these kinds of companies commonly reinvest their earnings into capital projects, research and development, or use them to acquire less-nimble competitors, most growth companies do not pay dividends. Many technology companies are within this niche.

Value stocks tend to grow more slowly and trade at lower prices relative to core measures like sales, earnings, or dividends. Most often, these stocks offer a higher dividend yield, lower price-to-book or price-to-sales ratios, and the balance sheets of the companies they represent show a significantly larger percentage of tangible assets than would those of the growth companies.

The stocks that make up the S&P 500® are selected by a committee. This is similar to the various Dow indexes. However, the S&P 500® Index also includes about a dozen non-US companies that are now incorporated outside of the US–or owned by foreign-based parent corporations–but were allowed to remain in the S&P 500® after their expatriation. Several other large foreign companies that have never been incorporated in the US, but whose shares trade on US exchanges, are part of the Index as well.

The committee selects the companies in the S&P 500® as representative of various industries in the US economy. Obviously, stocks that do not trade publicly (companies which are privately held) and those which have insufficient liquidity are not part of the Index. By contrast, the Fortune 500® Index seeks to list the five hundred largest public companies in the US by gross revenue, regardless of whether their stocks are easily traded, without consideration of their industry representation. Unlike the S&P 500®, however, it excludes companies incorporated outside the US.

> Most indexes are hard-wired to overlook bargains and overpay for wildly popular stocks.
>
> – Joel Greenblatt
> Gotham Capital

The S&P 500® Index was originally market-value weighted (the price of each stock multiplied by the number of shares issued by the company is the "market capitalization" or "market cap" of the company). In such a weighting scheme, the market caps are summed, and that total is divided by the number of stocks that make up the index. This methodology gives stocks of larger companies more impact on an index than companies whose market valuation is smaller.

Recently, the S&P 500® Index calculation method was changed to "float-weighted." Standard & Poor's determines the number of shares that are actually available for public trading, a number known as the *float*, and multiplies the float times the share price. These values are summed and the total divided by 500. This minimizes the impact of technology companies, which often have a large number of shares owned by employees but unavailable for trading, and minimizes the likelihood that another Internet or technology bubble could drive the Index to unsupportable levels. Nevertheless, the S&P 500® is still considered to be a market cap-weighted index, as opposed to the other possible measures, such as equal-weighted or fundamental-weighted based on a company's total economic footprint.

> Index funds are like horses with 20-pound jockeys running against ones carrying 200-pound jockeys.
>
> – Andrew Tobias

The NASDAQ Composite Index was launched in 1971 with a base value of 100. It is comprised of all the stocks listed on the NASDAQ (National Association of Securities Dealers Automated Quotation System) stock market–currently 2,895 components. It is widely followed in the US as an indicator of the performance of technology and growth stocks. Since both US and non-US companies are traded in the NASDAQ over-the-counter market, the index is not an exclusively American index. The index is calculated using market capitalization to weight each stock.

Yet another group of indexes is published by Russell Investments. In 1984, Russell recognized that the existing indexes, such as the DJIA and S&P 500®, did not represent the investments that most managers were making. In other words, the indexes were flawed (or biased), and this explained the inability of active managers to beat the market. The company developed new rules-based indexes to better measure the performance of what they termed "investable stocks." Their goal was to create a series of indexes that could be used as the basis for comparing the returns of mutual funds and other financial products.

Russell has been very successful, and many mutual funds, ETFs, and futures contracts are now tracked against their indexes. They also created indexes for global markets. Russell claims that more money is indexed using their benchmarks than any other index family.

Russell Investments' main US stock index is the Russell 3000®, which includes the leading 3,000 stocks as measured by market cap. The top 1,000 of those companies make up the large-cap Russell 1000®, and the remaining 2,000 smaller companies make up the small-cap Russell 2000®.

> A group of lemmings looks like a pack of individualists compared with Wall Street when it gets a concept in its teeth.
> – Warren Buffett

The Russell Global® Index reflects the performance of nearly 11,000 stocks worldwide, including the Russell 3000® as its US component and the Russell/Nomura Total Market Index as the Japanese component. Russell also publishes value and growth subsets of each US index. This divides each index approximately in half, separating companies classified as value stocks from those classified as growth stocks.

The humble origin of the stock market index more than 125 years ago (the Dow Jones Transportation Average, in 1884) provided a unique tool for forecasting and monitoring the economy. Since then, however, indexing has evolved into a powerful methodology for constructing myriad investment vehicles. By taking the guesswork out of selecting investments, indexes allow anyone to take advantage of Bogle's haystack maxim. Indexing allows an investor to select a particular slice of the US, international, or global economy in which to invest.

Ideally, we suggest investing in a group of indexes that provide an asset allocation with diverse domestic and global exposure. That approach is the at the core of the RVW method.

Weighting: The Inherent Hazard in Most of the Popular Indexes

In a move that rippled across the stock market, on Tuesday, April 5, 2011, Nasdaq OMX announced a rare rebalancing of its NASDAQ-100 index, which reduced the big weighting of Apple, Inc. At the time, the company made up more than 20% of the index. The rebalancing was driven in part by the seemingly unstoppable rise in Apple shares, which were up more than fourfold in the two prior years.

The tech company's big weighting means that a change in fortune for the maker of iPhones, iPods and iPads has a huge impact on one of the most heavily traded indexes in the market. In total, 81 of the 100 constituents of the index saw their share of the index reduced in the rebalancing.

The recent rebalancing of weightings within the NASDAQ-100 index, which took Apple stock from being 20% weighting of the index to 12%, illustrates *one of the significant problems with traditional indexing*. It was arbitrary and has no objective economic basis. "Because of the way the index has been calculated, Apple was given more than twice the weight in the index than it should have had based on its number of shares. Apple's market capitalization is roughly $300 billion, twice that of Google. But its weighting in the index was five times that of Google," wrote *The Wall Street Journal* of this change. "When the NASDAQ-100 was formed in 1985, it was comprised of the 100 biggest nonfinancial stocks listed in the NASDAQ Com-posite index based on their share prices and number of shares outstanding."

In an equal-weighted index fund, Apple would be 1% of the assets, as would each of the other 99 stocks.

Chapter 6
Exchange-Traded Funds: What Are They and Why Should I Consider Them?

> Investing is a science, not an art. The challenge is to adhere to the proven science of investing which works—and to overcome your compelling investment instincts that will invariably lead you astray.
> – Rip Van Winkle Wisdom

Exchange-Traded Funds (ETFs) are perhaps the most cost-efficient, tax-efficient, and liquid vehicles for index-based investing. They take the elegance and superior returns of traditional index mutual funds to the next level by packaging indexes into securities that trade just like stocks.

ETFs are a relatively recent creation of Wall Street. They are essentially baskets of stocks that trade together as one security. The vast majority of ETFs are passive index vehicles, designed to contain a predefined and objectively weighted group of securities. While actively managed ETFs are beginning to find their way into the marketplace, they remain a small piece of the ETF universe. ETFs, however, are an extraordinary story of successful financial innovation, having gone from nothing to over $1.5 trillion in assets in eighteen years in a universe of more than 3,000 funds.

The most notable difference between these investments and mutual funds is that open-end mutual funds typically trade only at the market's closing value (known as *forward pricing*), while ETFs trade continuously at their current *intraday* price. Moreover, ETFs can be sold short and are also optionable, meaning speculators can wager on future price movements without purchasing the ETF directly.

For RVW investors, index mutual funds are an excellent investment vehicle, but ETFs are superior in many ways and make what has always been a good idea even better. ETFs offer lower costs and greater tax-efficiency by eliminating the sometimes sizable phantom income taxes that can be created by mutual funds. As previously noted, an investor could purchase mutual fund shares in late-December and receive an IRS Form 1099 for the net realized taxable gains on that investment . . . even though he neither earned a penny nor made a trade after the acquisition. ETFs, on the other hand, pass virtually no income tax through to the investor. These and other advantages make ETFs ideal for long-term investing.

There have been many articles written comparing ETFs to index mutual funds, but most have been prepared by companies with an interest in the outcome of the debate. Mutual fund companies are able to show that their index funds are a better investment than ETFs. Not surprisingly, ETF sponsors manage to build a strong case for the superiority of index-based ETFs.

Who's right?

A large number of passive institutional investors prefer ETFs for their flexibility. Many prefer to use ETFs to hedge their stock market exposure instead of using more expensive futures and derivative contracts. Another advantage of ETFs is they may be purchased in smaller sizes than derivatives. They also don't require special accounts, incur no rollover costs, and may be bought and sold on margin. Additionally, some ETFs cover benchmarks where there are no futures contracts.

> Properly measured, the average actively managed dollar must underperform the average passively-managed dollar, net of costs. Empirical analyses that appear to refute this principle are guilty of improper measurement.
>
> – William F. Sharpe
> Nobel Laureate in Economics

Active traders, including hedge funds, trade ETFs for their convenience because they can be traded as easily as stocks. This means they have margin and trading flexibility unmatched by index mutual funds. Passive retail investors, for their part, often prefer index ETFs for their simplicity. Investors do not need a brokerage account to buy and hold index funds. They can often be purchased through the investor's own bank. This keeps things simple for investors. The reality, however, is that a brokerage account is no more difficult to open than a bank account and the brokerage account often includes features that would benefit the individual.

One of the original reasons for the creation of index funds was to lower the costs of investing. Bogle's vision was to closely mirror the market indexes, lagging by only a very small amount due to fund expenses. The investment community uses the term "tracking error" to describe how closely the mutual fund or ETF comes to matching the performance of the benchmark index.

ETFs are able to receive shares of stocks from very large investors, like pension funds, and this allows them to lower the costs of acquiring shares compared to mutual funds. Similarly, they can exchange shares with very large shareholders looking to close their ETF positions. While, this lowers costs only slightly, it is highly significant when it comes to tax-efficiency. By not actually selling or buying shares, typically there are no capital gains within the fund itself. These small savings in costs and substantial reductions in tax liabilities often add up to large gains over the long term. This advantage tips in favor of ETFs over mutual funds.

> I love index funds and ETFs. Index funds and ETFs are inexpensive to buy and own. They afford you immediate diversification, and they're extremely tax-efficient investments. Their performance is terrific and you aren't paying exorbitant fees to a fund manager. They're also very stable, meaning you don't have to worry about any unexpected changes a manager might make, or worry about the impact of a management change, or worry about winding up overexposed to any particular market sector.
>
> – Ben Stein, Economist and Humorist

To meet redemption requests, mutual funds need to maintain a certain amount of cash as part of their overall assets. In a rising market, holding cash lowers returns compared to being fully invested. This is not a concern of ETFs, which can quickly raise cash through the sale of stocks, futures or options contracts, or simply by borrowing from an investment bank for a short period of time.

Internal expenses, such as management fees and taxation, also favor ETFs. Operating expenses are generally lower for ETFs because they are not required to maintain individual records on each shareholder like mutual funds are required to do. The brokerage company you invest with incurs these costs on behalf of its ETF holders and builds them into their commission structure. Although the fund manager's fee represents the largest single expense of a mutual fund, mutual funds must necessarily spend a great deal of shareholder money complying with a variety of regulatory, reporting, and recordkeeping requirements.

Mutual fund shareholders can usually buy or sell index funds at no cost, but this is not the case for ETFs. Buying ETFs involves paying a commission to a broker. Using a discount online broker may cost as little as $5 or $10 per purchase–0.1% or less on a $10,000 investment, and even less on a percentage basis for larger investments. However, this is much less than continuous mutual fund management fees and is a small, one-time price pay to pay in order to obtain those savings.

In general, ETFs are suitable for those who prefer to take a buy-and-hold approach because the upfront commissions can be amortized over a long holding period. Mutual funds, on the other hand, may offer a better way for those who tend to hold for shorter periods because there is generally no entrance or exit fee for no-load mutual funds.

In his seminal work, *Index Mutual Funds and Exchange-Traded Funds*, Leonard Kostovetsky attempts to objectively quantify the differences between ETFs and index mutual funds. According to his analysis, with a long-term horizon of at least ten-years, an investor with at least $13,000 is better served taking a position in ETFs than in index mutual funds; the larger the amount invested, the shorter the break-even period.

Another advantage of ETFs is your ability to utilize the many options available to develop the right asset allocation strategy for your financial circumstances. There are many more options available through ETFs compared to index mutual funds to match the multiple financial demands that individual investors face. You can design a portfolio with ETFs to achieve a value or growth tilt, emphasize small-cap or large-cap investments, and even attain a desired amount of global stock market exposure. This process ensures exactly the right balance of risk and reward to match your needs.

> ETFs are likely to continue their assault on the traditional turf of mutual funds. During the past decade, ETFs have grown steadily. ETF assets totaled $1.1 trillion in July this year, up 23 percent from the year before . . . . Much of the growth can be traced to advisors who have been enthusiastic users of ETFs. . . . Of RIAs who oversee $250 million to $1 billion in assets, 99 percent use ETFs.
>
> – Stan Luxenberg, Writer
> *Investing/Fund Watch*
> *Registered Rep.*, October 2011

The inherent nature of ETFs also mitigates against the "style drift" that can adversely affect mutual fund investors. Typically defined as "the divergence of a mutual fund from its stated investment style or objective," style drift most often results from the direct effect of portfolio investing decisions by the fund manager and his team, a change in the fund's management, or simply the growth of an underlying company within the fund's holdings.

Although style drift is not always disadvantageous to an investor, the most likely result is diminished returns over time. As has already been said, fund managers who spend their time chasing performance may resort to using short-term strategies which are often counterproductive and can dramatically alter the expected risk-return profile of the fund.

Still, there is no bright line that distinguishes the benefits of owning index mutual funds from index ETFs, and investors who own shares of index mutual funds are more likely to fare better over the long haul compared to those who own other funds that are actively managed–and especially so when compared to their peers who continually seek the returns of the next hot fund they see in their rear-view mirror. But, clearly, there are several distinct advantages to owning ETFs for the long-term investor, without regard for the size of their investment, which are not available to mutual fund shareholders and cannot be ignored.

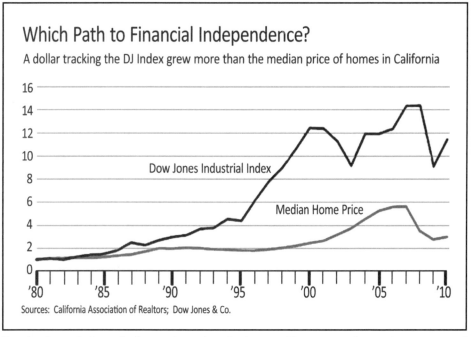

Which Path to Financial Independence?

A dollar tracking the DJ Index grew more than the median price of homes in California

Dow Jones Industrial Index

Median Home Price

Sources: California Association of Realtors; Dow Jones & Co.

Despite the turbulence in the stock markets in the past 30 years, stocks continue to reward investors with superior returns compared to real estate.

Chapter 7
There's a Hole in the Bucket:
Why Active Investors Get Lousy Returns

> If you pay the executives at Sarah Lee more, it doesn't make the cheesecake less good. But with mutual funds, it comes directly out of the batter.
>
> – Don Phillips, President
> Morningstar, Inc.

Most investors don't realize how multiple layers of fees and tax inefficiencies eat away at their portfolio returns. Active managers frequently pursue gains with little regard for the best interests of their investors.

Arguably, mutual funds are managed by some of the brightest minds on Wall Street. These "professional money managers" approach their work each day with the best of intentions, and are sincerely motivated to deliver the best returns possible consistent with the investment objectives of the fund. Unfortunately, most cannot overcome the handicap imposed by their funds' high cost structures necessary to match the market.

When discussing the virtues of mutual fund investing, your investment advisor is very likely to bring up the miracle of compounding. You will be shown the value of investing for the long term and how important it is to let your money work for you. These are all valid points and are also illustrated in this book. However, most investment advisors conveniently leave out the rest of the story–what John Bogle refers to as the "tyranny of compounding costs"–which is, simply, the fact that *fees and taxes accumulated over long periods significantly reduce your wealth*.

One seemingly small cost is the expense fund managers incur to buy and sell the thousands of shares they trade every day. Trading commissions may amount to just a fraction of a penny per share . . . but these transaction costs add up over time. Mutual fund managers trade huge lots of shares and all those pennies add up. While an individual transaction cost may seem insignificant, taken as a whole, they detract from the performance of the fund.

Morningstar studied this problem and found that the average annual turnover ratio for actively managed domestic stock funds is 130%, implying that the average fund holds a stock for about nine months. Another way to state this: The manager is trading $1.30 for every dollar invested in the fund.

However it is described, all that activity costs money, and it's the investor who ultimately foots the bill. The Bogle Financial Markets Research Center also looked at average mutual fund returns with an eye toward figuring out what all this means to the typical investor. They found that hyperactive trading lowered annualized returns about 0.7%.

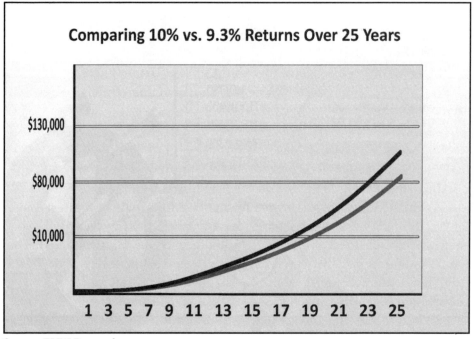

Source: RVW Research

Figure 7-1: Small costs add up over time. Paying less than 1% a year in commissions can reduce your total profits by more than 15% over twenty-five years.

Sacrificing less than 1% per year seems small, but over twenty-five years it could negatively impact your wealth by more than 15%. This idea is shown in Figure 7-1. A $10,000 investment grows to more than $108,000 with an average annual return of 10%, but is only slightly more than $92,000 at 9.3%. This difference of nearly $16,000 is the direct impact of the manager's trading activity and the expense that generates.

There is also "opportunity cost" that must be accounted for, since very few stocks are likely to reach their full potential in less than a year. While always seeking next month's winner, fund managers are often selling stocks that might be big gainers over time. They may buy back stocks they previously sold, but usually after missing out on gains and certainly after incurring trading costs. This is another reason to avoid active managers in favor of pure index investment strategies.

The impact of the tyranny of compounding is fully illustrated by

Bogle in The Little Book of Common Sense Investing. In his example, he assumes, conservatively, that the stock market will deliver a modest annual return of 8% over fifty years. An actively managed mutual fund will lag that by the cost of expenses, which he assumes to be 2.5% per year. Obtaining market returns of 8% results in a $10,000 investment growing to $469,000, while the mutual fund, with its returns of only 5.5% per year, grows to just $145,400. The difference–an astounding $323,600–is the cost to the investor for active management. Figure 7-2 shows that after just ten years an investor receives only 79% of the market returns, but after fifty years, barely 31% of the possible returns have accrued to the investor.

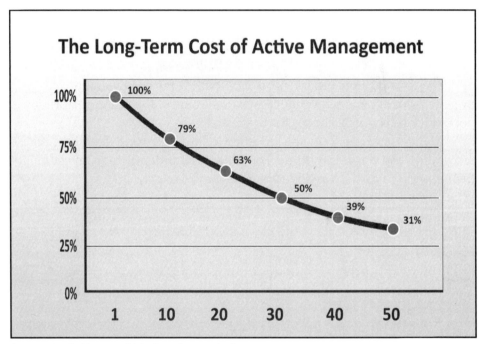

The Long-Term Cost of Active Management

Source: Bogle Financial Markets Research Center

Figure 7-2: Total returns drop off dramatically with each decade. The average expenses associated with an actively managed mutual fund can reduce your returns dramatically over time, when compared to a passive, index-based investment approach.

Another unseen but substantial cost is associated with taxes. SmartMoney magazine calculated that as a result of capital gains and other taxable distributions, mutual fund investors would pay nearly $32 billion in taxes for 2007 . . . without selling a single share! Because these gains are distributed to all shareholders, the buy-and-hold investor often faces a hefty tax bill–in good times and in bad. Actual performance has nothing to do with distributions, since they are based on tax accounting rather than the posted returns.

In her April 2008 *SmartMoney* article, *The Worst Kind of Surprise–A Tax Hit*, writer Janet Paskin calculates that the average investor loses 2.3% per year to taxes, a loss of $5,000 over the first ten years of a $10,000 investment. And it compounds to some $24,000 over the next ten years!

> When active managers boast their fund's returns, savvy investors ought to deduct about 2% to determine a comparable return when reviewing their passive, index-based portfolios.
>
> – Rip Van Winkle Wisdom

When you add it all up, fund-generated fees account for a large part of the underperformance of actively managed mutual funds. Burton G. Malkiel, author of *A Random Walk Down Wall Street*, notes that "funds have underperformed benchmark portfolios both after management fees and even gross of expenses." While fees explain part of the underperformance, poor stock selection accounts for the rest.

Malkiel summed up the question of mutual fund fees in a single sentence: "The data do not give one much confidence that investors get their money's worth from investment advisory expenditures."

> Wall Street is the land of the brave and the home of the fee.
>
> – Rip Van Winkle Wisdom

Chapter 8
Beyond Traditional Indexes

> While much has changed over the years, some things remain the same. There is still a strong relation between risk and expected return, and price-scaled fundamental variables (such as book-to-market) still have explanatory power for stock returns. Some things have stood the test of time.
>
> – James L. Davis, Author
> *Digging the Panama Canal*

Equal-weighted and fundamental-weighted indexes have distinct advantages over more established capitalization-weighted indexes. ETFs based upon these simple strategies can protect investors from fad stocks and achieve steadier returns over time.

Research has consistently demonstrated that markets work. Markets around the world have a proven history of rewarding investors for their investments. The inherent problem is that most individuals compete with each other to find the most attractive returns, trying to select the companies that will offer the best returns within a market. This competition between investors ensures that prices will remain pretty close to their fair value, meaning that no individual investor should expect greater returns than average without taking on greater-than-average risk.

Active investment managers are all attempting to outperform the market by finding stocks they believe are mispriced. In other words, they are trying to predict the future by guessing which stocks will go up more than the overall market. The majority of the time, this proves costly and futile. Predictions are usually wrong, and these errors lead active managers to miss the strong returns that markets often provide only because they are caught holding the wrong stocks at the wrong time. As has been demonstrated, randomly throwing darts at the newspaper's list of available stocks to create a one-year portfolio has a greater likelihood of success than most active stock-picking.

The fact that successful short-term speculation is nearly impossible is good news for the long-term investor. It means that market prices for stocks are fair and that differences in total returns can be explained by differences in risk. This leads to the natural conclusion that it is certainly possible to outperform the market, but only by accepting increased risk.

Academic studies point to one inescapable conclusion–returns are tied to risk. This applies in the markets just as it does in every other aspect of life. Gains are rarely, if ever, accomplished without taking a chance. Numerous studies have analyzed market trends attempting to identify which financial risks are worth taking and which are not.

> Elephants don't gallop, horses do. Stock prices of large companies with big capitalizations move up and down slowly relative to smaller companies because there is less market ignorance and uncertainty for big companies to profit from. Smaller companies are inherently more risky. Over time, buying smaller companies therefore tends to be far more rewarding. Risk and reward are generally two sides of the same coin.
>
> – Rip Van Winkle Wisdom

In general, the studies conclude that two factors can be employed to consistently achieve above-market returns. First, small-company stocks have higher expected returns than large-company stocks and, second, value stocks have higher expected returns than growth stocks. Many analysts believe that small-cap and value stocks outperform most other classes of stocks because they have greater underlying risks. Small companies are more likely to go out of business than large companies, for example, and value stocks may be low-priced because the companies have fallen on hard times and may not recover. The lower prices offer investors greater upside rewards as compensation for taking on the added risk of loss.

Risk is rewarded over time. Over the long term, small-cap stocks have outperformed large-cap stocks by an average of more than two percentage points annually. The results are shown in Figure 8-1. A $1 investment in small-cap value stocks would have returned an average of 13.6% and grown to more than $39,299 over the eighty-three years ending in 2010. That same $1 invested in large-cap value stocks instead would have grown to just over $3,518, an average annual return of 10.3% per year.

The different rates of return are even greater when growth and value investing methodologies are factored into the analysis. There are two general investment styles, one value and the other growth, both of which dominate the mutual fund industry and account for a large part of stock market trading. Value investors look for stocks that they believe are trading at less than their intrinsic values, selecting those with lower-than-average price-to-book or price-to-earnings ratios, or which may offer high dividend yields. Growth investors seek out stocks of companies they think will enjoy a strong future, whose earnings are expected to grow at a faster rate compared to their particular sector or compared to the market as a whole.

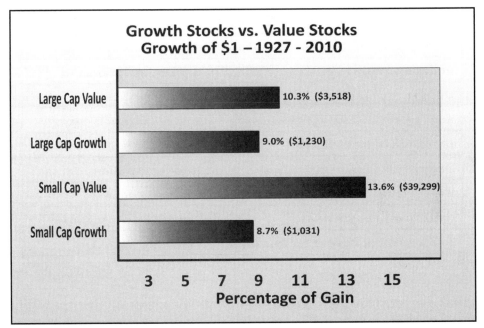

Source: RVW Research

Figure 8-1: Small-cap stocks deliver greater returns than large-cap stocks over time. Although they carry greater risk than their large-cap counterparts, investments made in small-cap stocks reward investors handsomely in the long run. Value stocks are those which tend to be underpriced when compared to the overall stock market.

For most investors, the US stock market represents the first equity asset class in a diversified portfolio. Sometimes it represents the only equity exposure for an individual investor. Individuals can usually do better by adding international markets to their portfolio. Consistent with the idea that small-caps do better, European, Asian, and developing markets are all smaller than the US market. In Figure 8-2, we see that these markets offer a large investment opportunity.

Global stock market exposure allows investors to participate in the success of some of the best-known companies. Many household names are actually companies from outside the US (Table 8-1), companies that prudent investors should own.

The data support the idea that these smaller markets do better than the larger US market over time. In Figure 8-3, on page 96, we see that over nineteen years, these emerging markets nearly doubled the investment returns available from the large-cap indexes of the US market.

GLOBAL INDUSTRIAL POWERHOUSES

BP (GASOLINE)	LONDON, ENGLAND
SAMSUNG (CONSUMER ELECTRONICS)	SEOUL, SOUTH KOREA
ING (INSURANCE, FINANCIAL SERVICES)	AMSTERDAM, NETHERLANDS
ADIDAS (ATHLETIC FOOTWEAR, CLOTHING)	HERZOGENAURACH, GERMANY
ROLEX (WATCHES)	GENEVA, SWITZERLAND
L'OREAL (COSMETICS)	CLICHY, FRANCE
SONY (ELECTRONICS & ENTERTAINMENT)	TOKYO, JAPAN
BAYER (PHARMACEUTICALS)	LEVERKUSEN, GERMANY
TOYOTA (AUTOMOBILES)	TOYOTA CITY, AICHI, JAPAN
BARCLAYS (FINANCIAL SERVICES)	LONDON, ENGLAND
IKEA (HOME FURNISHINGS)	LEIDEN, NETHERLANDS
NESTLE (FOOD, BEVERAGE, PHARMA)	VEVEY, SWITZERLAND

Table 8-1: Global companies that produce many of the best-known products are a required part of a well-diversified portfolio.

Developed markets may also offer better returns than the US market, as illustrated below in Table 8-2. The advantage of adding global investments to your portfolio is that by introducing non-correlated risk, you can reduce the overall portfolio volatility. By taking advantage of opportunities abroad, you may experience higher returns than if you invested solely in the US market. In any given year, it is impossible to predict which market will be the top performer, so it is important to take a diversified approach.

	US GROWTH	BEST DEVELOPED MARKET	GROWTH
2007	5%	AUSTRALIA	27%
2008	-31%	JAPAN	-33%
2009	29%	AUSTRALIA	66%
2010	49%	FINLAND	23%

Source: RVW Research

Table 8-2: Global investing offers growth that may beat the US market. The US will rarely be the best performing market in the world, and the returns from well-developed economies often dwarf US stocks.

The risks of global investing, just like the returns, are usually non-correlated with the US market. There are unique risks, like currency fluctuations, foreign taxation, global economic and political risks, and differences in accounting and financial standards, associated with investing in foreign markets.

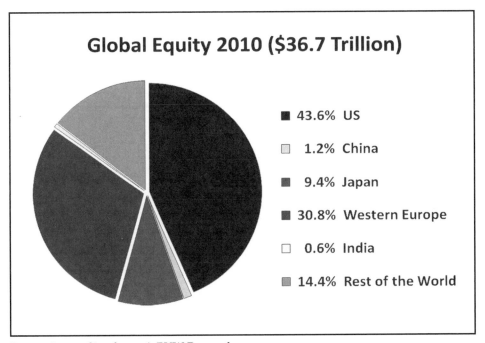

Global Equity 2010 ($36.7 Trillion)

- 43.6% US
- 1.2% China
- 9.4% Japan
- 30.8% Western Europe
- 0.6% India
- 14.4% Rest of the World

Source: JeremySiegel.com & RVW Research

Figure 8-2: More than half of the world's stock market capitalization lies outside the US China and India, although growing fast, have economies that are insignificant when compared to the developed nations.

Some would argue that tilting a portfolio toward a particular sector of the market, such as small-company stocks or value stocks, is the same as stock-picking, which is a loser's game. But if there's more than one type of risk driving returns, and all studies agree that there are multiple risk factors impacting stocks, it is possible for investors to gain greater expected returns. They do this by using a wider range of strategies while remaining within the bounds of indexing.

Newer indexes, available as ETFs, take advantage of these academic studies and allow for gains that beat the market. Equal-weighted indexes provide broad exposure to all companies in an index such as the S&P 500® without allowing a small group of larger stocks to dominate the performance of the investment. An equal-weighted index buys each of the 500 stocks in equal amounts, compared to the traditional index fund or ETF which holds each company in proportion to its capitalization within the index. By eliminating the bias large companies, an equal-weighted index provides investors with the opportunity to outperform the index with lower volatility.

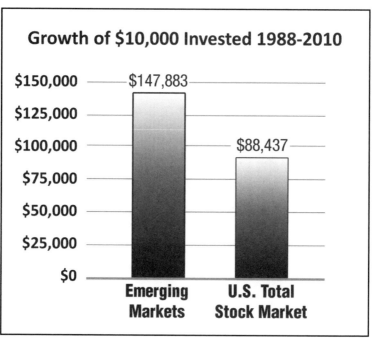

Source: RVW Research

Figure 8-3: Emerging markets offer greater returns and greater risks to US investors. Again, we see that investors willing and able to bear risk are usually amply rewarded over time.

Equal-weighted ETFs offer an alternative to traditional cap-weighted index investments. The equal-weighting approach invests across both an index's market segments and its constituent components. As a result, each component of the index is represented equally, whether at the constituent or sector level or both. For these reasons, the equal-weight strategy provides at least three potential benefits to investors, including:

1. **Broader Diversification.** While diversification cannot promise a profit or prevent a loss, it does seek to reduce the risk of concentration in the portfolio's holdings and balance the portfolio's exposure across the broader sectors, market capitalizations, and other risk factors.

2. **Performance.** The main feature of equal-weighting is the reduction of bias toward the larger companies that comprise an index. Smaller-company stocks frequently outperform those of large companies, especially when large caps are

disfavored. However, ETFs may not perform as well as their benchmarks when large caps are favored.

3. **Disciplined Rebalancing.** Regularly rebalancing a portfolio locks in the profit from those components outperforming the benchmark and reinvests it among the components that are underperforming in order to bring the portfolio's weighting back to equilibrium, maintaining the neutral bias toward all constituents of the index. Ideally, this strategy will both balance and reduce portfolio risk factors.

Figure 8-4 shows that the theory behind equal-weighted indexing works. Frequent rebalancing to prevent one sector from dominating the index provides steadier increasing gains. Over five years, the equal-weighted index provided an additional 1% per year on average. In dollar terms, a $10,000 investment in a traditional cap-weighted index increased to about $15,000 over the five years ending in 2007. That same investment in an equal-weighted index would have grown to more than $18,000.

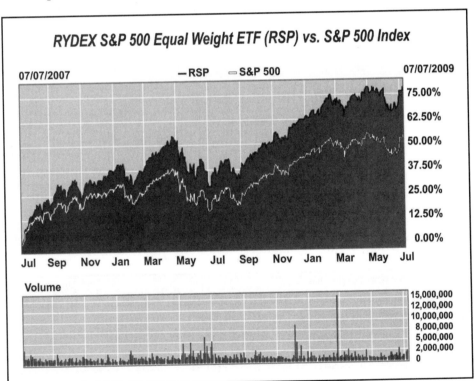

Source: RVW Research

Figure 8-4: An equal-weighted index delivers higher returns in this example. This figure demonstrates the value of buying low and selling high, which is the rebalancing discipline followed by equal-weighted indexes.

Other ETFs have been developed to address the finding that value investment strategies generally outpace growth strategies in the long term. The problem with traditional indexing is that as investing fads gain steam, the index becomes top-heavy with stocks that have become overvalued. This comes at the expense of underweighting lower-valued securities, the ones most likely to perform best in the future. The result is that capitalization- and float-weighted indexes are at a disadvantage to the equal-weighted indexes. Equal-weighting requires the manager to follow the discipline of "buy low and sell high," thus enhancing future returns.

Additional studies demonstrate that fundamental-indexing, which is based on standard stock market measures, also performs better than cap-weighted indexing. The Fundamental Index, a proprietary technique of Research Affiliates, LLC, based in Newport Beach, CA, and the team of researchers, led by Robert Arnott and Jason Hsu, Ph.D., seeks to assign weightings within an index-based ETF. They assign the weightings by relying on the actual economic footprint of the enterprise. A variety of accounting items, including sales, dividends, cash flow, and book value, offer the prospect of increased returns. ETFs are available that select and weight securities using these fundamental values to break the long-standing limitations of standard indexing. The results are shown in Table 8-3.

Value Factors Enhance Returns

	GROWTH OF $1 FROM 1962-2006	ANNUAL RETURN	ANNUAL VOLATILITY
S&P 500	$85	10.38%	14.74%
HIGH DIVIDEND YIELD	$166	12.04%	13.39%
LOW PRICE-TO-BOOK RATIO	$177	12.19%	14.64%
LOW PRICE-TO-CASH FLOW RATIO	$207	12.95%	14.53%
LOW PRICE-TO-SALES RATIO	$204	12.59%	15.53%

Source: Research Affiliates, LLC

Table 8-3: These returns demonstrate the benefits of a value indexing methodology.

Figure 8-5 demonstrates how ETFs that employ alternative asset allocation strategies have outperformed the best-performing cap-weighted index funds. These alternative strategies all use methods that ignore the cap-weighting approach that marks the S&P 500® and other major indexes, such as the Russell 1000.

Buying value stocks also makes a significant difference. All approaches nearly double the total returns with about the same amount of risk. An ETF using these strategies would also hold fewer stocks than a traditional index ETF, resulting in lower transaction costs and greater tax efficiency.

Combining the latest in research with indexing strategies allows investors to improve on the market return without trying to pick the best stocks or the best managers. These techniques deliver on the promise of active management without the costs and the risks usually associated with an active manager.

> Surprises are for birthdays, not for tax time.
> – Rip Van Winkel Wisdom

From year-to-year it is impossible to predict which asset class will have the best performance. This is why broad diversification is critical for investment success.

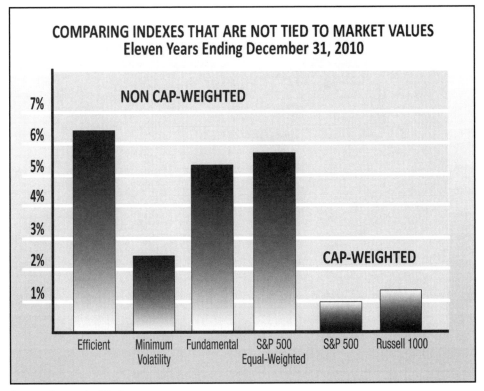

Source: Journal of Indexes

Figure 8-5: Index funds outperformed the market in the last decade, but many ETFs far outperformed the best-known index funds over the same period of time.

Chapter 9
Diversification:
The Key to Managing Risk

> Diversification is when the ice cream man branches into selling ponchos.
> – Rip Van Winkle Wisdom

Successful investors have a variety of investments in their portfolios, which often includes ETFs based on international and domestic stocks with varying styles. The well-diversified portfolio also includes a mix of bonds. Proper asset allocation is driven by personal circumstances, not simplistic formulas. It is also important to rebalance the portfolio at regular intervals to maintain the intended diversification.

Diversification results in the allocation of your total investment portfolio between different types of investments, including stocks, bonds, real estate, and a limited amount of cash. Investors should also be diversified into different investment strategies within those broad categories. Using mutual funds or ETFs for the stock portion of a portfolio might mean owning a selection of growth, value, small-cap, large-cap, and sector elements. Geographic diversification can be achieved by owning a combination of international and domestic investments.

It has long been established by the academic community that diversification significantly reduces risk in a portfolio. In 1952, Harry Markowitz published a paper titled *Portfolio Selection*. He was later awarded the Nobel Prize in Economics for his work which began with this research. Markowitz developed the idea of selecting stocks to maximize returns given an individual's tolerance for risk. He provided the math to justify the common sense notion that widows and orphans should hold more conservative investments than a thirty-something multimillionaire.

Markowitz stressed the need to think of individual stocks as part of a portfolio. He demonstrated that performance depended upon balancing risk and reward. It is possible to balance riskier stocks and safer stocks within a portfolio to provide solid returns and thereby achieve less risk than seen in the overall market. In other words, with proper diversification, an investor should be able to beat the market by holding a well-diversified portfolio. This portfolio approach results in less risk than owning the total market, despite the fact that within the portfolio there are individual elements that have relatively higher risk.

Figure 9-1 shows the relationship between portfolio volatility, as measured by standard deviation, and the number of asset classes in a portfolio. The mathematical concept of standard deviation usually refers to a measure of risk for any investment. The higher the standard deviation, the more a series of data varies from its average. In the case of stocks, price history with a higher standard deviation would be considered to be more volatile than an investment option which has a lower standard deviation. Because most investors prefer to see steady gains, associating volatility with risk means standard deviation is also a measure of risk.

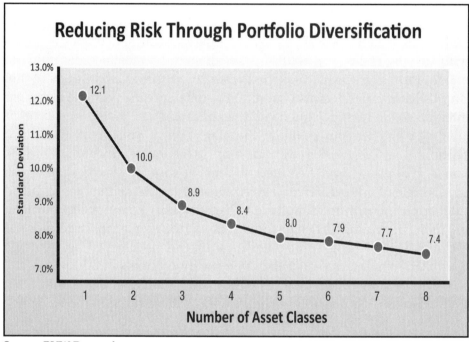

Source: RVW Research

Figure 9-1: An illustration of the idea that "The essence of effective portfolio construction is the use of a large number of poorly correlated assets."– William Bernstein, *The Intelligent Asset Allocator*.

In Figure 9-1, the different asset classes include a variety of stock indexes, various measures of bond performance, and real estate. It becomes more obvious that risk steadily declines as the portfolio becomes more diversified.

Another example of standard deviation might be helpful to illustrate this idea. Consider two stock portfolios, each of which finishes the second year with total gains of about 25%. Both portfolios begin with a value of $1,000 and end up increasing in value to $1,250. The monthly returns are shown in Figure 9-2.

Most investors would prefer the steady gains of 1% per month shown by the red line. While both investors end up with the same account value, the investment performance represented by the blue line arrives there by giving back a significant amount of profits along the way. In hindsight, the loss on paper hurts just as much, if not more, than realized losses: "If only I had sold that when . . . ." Having invested in a mutual fund whose manager achieved the blue line returns, you might even feel like you lost money during the year.

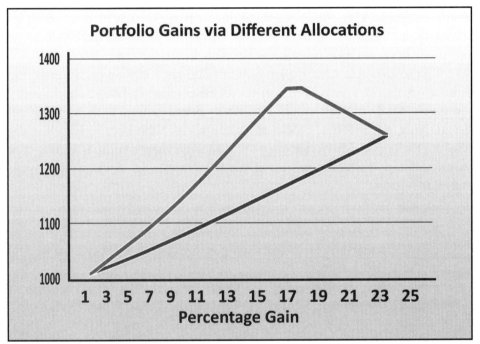

Source: RVW Research

Figure 9-2: While both investors reach the same end point, they arrive by sharply different paths. The bottom line represents slow but steady growth. The top line shows that winning streaks always come to an end.

This graphic portrayal comparing the sequence of gains illustrates well the idea that investors tend to prefer lower volatility when it comes to returns. This observation is confirmed mathematically by calculating the standard deviations of the monthly returns. The gain achieved with a steady 1% per month return shown by the lower line has a standard deviation of 79, significantly lower than the standard deviation of 111 for the upper line.

From this relatively simple example, we can see that standard deviation can serve well as a measurement of risk. Steadier gains are preferable to most investors, and the steadier the gains the lower the standard deviation.

> Savvy investors embrace risk and recognize that it is the source of their superior returns. The key is to quantify risk, manage it, diversify it, and be patient.
> – Rip Van Winkle Wisdom

The concept of diversification limits the impact of any single stock or asset class by spreading risk across a combination of asset classes. As a result, declines in the total returns of one or two assets is usually offset by increases in others. In Figure 9-1, as the number of investment classes in the portfolio increases, the overall risk decreases.

It is impossible to completely eliminate risk. However, diversifying your investments among noncorrelated asset classes should significantly reduce the total volatility of your portfolio. Some general rules apply when diversifying a portfolio. Stocks carry more risk than bonds, which is the reason stocks provide better long-term returns than bonds. It is also true that small-cap stocks are more volatile than large-cap stocks and provide superior returns.

> Over 90 percent of investment returns are determined by how investors allocate their assets versus security selection, market-timing, and other factors.
> – Gary P. Brinson, Brian D. Singer, and Gilbert L. Beebower
> "Determinants of Portfolio Performance II: An Update,"
> *Financial Analysts Journal* (47:3, May-June 1991)

International securities involve more risk for the US investor than an investment in the US markets. Changes in currency, particularly the long-term decline in the value of the US dollar, has a significant impact on the returns realized by Americans investing abroad. In emerging markets, which offer the greatest potential returns, political instability is another risk factor that cannot be easily quantified. For these and other reasons, the returns achieved from international stock investments exceed the returns from US stocks *over the long term*. Substantial short-term volatility will be also be seen.

The idea of risk and reward is easily illustrated and shown in Table 9-1. For this example, we use an S&P 500® index fund to represent stocks, and a long-term government bond fund. We vary the allocations and find the returns for those portfolios over the test period, which begins in July

1991 and runs through June 2011, a full twenty years.

% STOCKS	% BONDS	AVERAGE RETURN	MAXIMUM DRAWDOWN
100	0	10.1%	−45%
80	20	10.2%	−33%
50	50	10.2%	− 9%
20	80	10.0%	−10%
0	100	9.7%	−16%

Source: RVW Research

Table 9-1: The 50/50 mix of stocks and bonds offers the best returns with the least risk. In all cases, adding bonds to the portfolio decreases overall risk.

Combining the different risks and rewards can lead to a portfolio where the sum is greater than the combination of the parts. While it seems counterintuitive, a 50/50 mix of bonds and stocks outperformed either stocks or bonds alone and with less risk ("drawdown"). While the difference in returns seen in the 50/50 portfolio allocation is minimal, the risk reduction is most dramatic. The lowest returns are found in a 100% bond portfolio.

Risk will be reduced more than returns by adding bonds to the stock portfolio. Reducing one's exposure to stocks by only 20% lowers risk by more than 10% and increases returns by 0.1%. Most investors will sleep better at night with less risk, and the peace of mind is worth the price paid in foregone returns.

> The two ends of a see-saw are negatively correlated; they move in opposite directions. The swing and the see-saw are noncorrelated. They move totally independent of each other.
> – Rip Van Winkle Wisdom

The idea behind diversification is that when one asset moves down, another is likely to move up. This is called *noncorrelation*–when the various assets in a portfolio do not all move in the same direction simultaneously. Not only do stocks and bonds tend to move in opposite directions (negatively correlated), small-company stocks and large-company stocks do not always move in lock-step (noncorrelated).

The biggest challenge with diversification is that it requires some effort to maintain the asset allocation at the intended percentages. While many investors initially create a diversified portfolio, over time the performance of one asset may result in too much weight in the portfolio. After performing well enough to grow in size, it is likely to underperform for some time. Unless the portfolio is periodically and systematically rebalanced, the large gains will inadvertently be allowed to slip away.

Over the course of a year, or perhaps even just six months, a portfolio that started out as 60% stocks and 40% bonds can easily become 50/50 as the prices of stocks decline and those of bonds rise or, *vice versa*, to 70% stocks and 30% bonds if stock prices rise and bond prices decline. Rebalancing means there will always be a need to periodically sell some of the winners and buy more of the laggards to bring the allocation back to the starting point. Reward is found by locking in gains and increasing investment in the part of the portfolio likely to benefit from long-term shifts in the market place. Failure to routinely rebalance the portfolio on a regular basis is likely to result in an unintended failure in the maintenance of the desired allocation, increasing risk unnecessarily.

Table 9-2 demonstrates what can happen to a portfolio over twenty years without periodic rebalancing. The percentages measure the sum of asset values, not the quantity of assets, in the portfolio.

	% STOCKS	% BONDS
1987	50	50
1997	69	31
2007	73	27

Source: RVW Research

Table 9-2: Over a relatively short period of time, a balanced portfolio can become dramatically over-weighted towards stocks.

In order to maintain the asset allocation strategy within the portfolio, investors and their advisors should review their holdings at least once a year. Ideally, whenever asset allocations have drifted by more than 5% from the desired target, rebalancing is required. This is done by selling assets which have appreciated and buying more of those that are underperforming. Rebalancing is a disciplined approach to buying low and selling high. It results in the portfolio acting in accordance with sound, well-researched principles of investing, emphasizing the science rather than the art.

One way to diversify your portfolio is to increase the number of its holdings. Table 9-3 on the next page illustrates this concept. While increasing the number of stocks lowers risk, it is unrealistic to believe that eliminating all risk is a possibility. There will always be risk associated with being invested in the stock market. The easiest way to increase the number of stocks in a portfolio is by owning mutual funds or ETFs.

An additional way to increase diversification and reduce risk is to simply use time as your investment ally (see Figure 9-3). The longer you hold your investment, the more the risk and volatility of portfolio returns will be reduced through proper diversification.

Unfortunately, there are no hard-and-fast rules to define either proper diversification or the proper time frame for rebalancing your portfolio. These decisions demand an understanding of both your personal investment needs and consideration of your tax situation. No matter what your circumstances are, the only certainty is diversification and rebalancing are very likely to improve your investment performance.

NUMBER OF STOCKS IN PORTFOLIO	PERCENTAGE OF STOCK & SECTOR RISK ELIMINATED
2	46%
4	72%
8	81%
16	93%
32	96%
64	98%
500	99%
ALL STOCKS	100%

Source: Institute for Econometric Research & RVW Research

Table 9-3: Increasing the number of holdings decreases risk.

People have to be brave and step into the market. Yes, there will be some periods of slumps. There may even be some periods of extremely prolonged slumps, and there is always a chance that you could lose a lot of money in a downturn too (on paper, certainly, or in actuality if other circumstances forced a person to have to sell). But, all in all, *and over time,* the broad market indexes are much more likely than not to provide a considerably better return on your money.

Sure, it can be scary sometimes, but as we have seen, whenever the US stock market goes down, you have some very, very smart people, like Warren Buffett, who are diligently buying stocks, putting significant sums of money *into* the market. In fact, during the extreme market turmoil surrounding the debt-ceiling "crisis" in Washington, DC, in early-August 2011, Buffet quietly invested some *$3 billion* on the day the Dow plunged

more than 500 points. His Berkshire Hathaway fund reportedly held close
to $15 billion in cash at the time–poised for just such a buying opportunity.

Good times teach only bad lessons: that investing is easy, that you
know its secrets, and that you needn't worry about risk.
                        – Howard Marks
                        Oaktree Capital

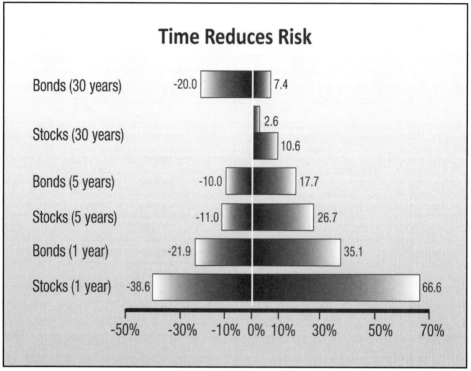

Time Reduces Risk

Source: JeremySiegel.com & RVW Research

Figure 9-3: The variability of stock returns diminishes markedly over time, actually
decreasing the chance of losses. When adjusted for inflation, bonds retain their riskiness
over all time frames. Younger people, however, have the great advantage of time.

Of course, not everyone is well-served through putting a lot of their
money into the stock market. If you're already a senior, this might not be a
good idea at all. For example, an eighty three-year-old retiree will be much
better off keeping his money liquid in CDs or money market accounts than
looking for a safe and steady 5% annual increase. Even putting one's money
into a broad market index fund could be too risky for an older person's
situation. Although life expectancy at age eighty-three is another twelve or

thirteen years, time is no longer on the side of market risk. The investor's other assets, sources of income, state of health, and lifestyle considerations all need to be taken into account.

> If you don't want to take risks, you can't expect too much in the way of rewards. The reason you get returns greater than you would otherwise get from having your money in a money market fund or a Treasury bond is because there is that risk component to the stock market. And so the very reason some folks complain about and use to justify their not putting money into the stock market is the exact same reason why it pays off better than the less risky investments.
> – Ben Stein, Economist and Humorist

As we have already seen, the earlier one invests, the greater the effect of compounding over time. For a younger person, investing the bulk of his or her money in "safe investments" now comes with two very significant risks that cannot be minimized: inflation risk and longevity risk. Very young persons (those under thirty-five, perhaps), should position most all of their invested money in stocks, because they have the longest time frame before beginning to draw down their investments–and have sufficient time to wait for markets to recover from any declines. The greatest danger is to be forced to sell off equity investments during a bear market. Only as one becomes older will the need for more liquidity become apparent–and accomplished by positioning more money into bonds, money market funds, or CDs.

There is no reason to fear the stock market. No other opportunity has provided investors with the long-term consistency of returns seen in the stock market–not gold, diamonds, or real estate. So prepare to take the plunge by getting your feet wet today, and watch your wealth begin to increase–*as you sleep tight at night.*

Chapter 10
Understanding Investor Behavior
(or, Why Your First Response
Is Likely the Wrong Investment Decision)

> In investing, what is comfortable is rarely profitable.
>
> – Robert Arnott, Investment Manager

Investors respond to many situations in predictably irrational ways. These self-sabotaging behaviors can be avoided . . . if you know what to look for.

Most financial theory is based on the assumption that individuals act rationally. Researchers have studied real people making real decisions about money and discovered that most people can, indeed, behave irrationally.

An academic discipline known as *behavioral economics* has emerged out of that research. Specialists in behavioral economics study individual psychology and group dynamics as they try to understand what motivates people to make financial decisions ranging from at which grocery store to shop to in which stock to invest for their retirement. Many researchers have come to believe that irrational financial decisions can actually be predicted.

Paul Slovic, a University of Oregon psychologist and authority on how we assess risk, comes close to summarizing this body of knowledge into a single sentence: "Most people just can't think about risk in an analytic way. The average person goes by gut feelings."

There are four key findings associated with this research:

1. SURVIVAL INSTINCT. The basic survival instinct that ensures one's success in most other endeavors in life is the result of millions of years of genetic adaptations. Unfortunately, it can lead the average investor to sell at precisely the wrong time–in the midst of market panics. The typical reaction in a downturn is to panic and sell–even though the risk is actually far lower than it was when stocks were higher. When all appears gloomy and dangerous, the survival instinct compels us to action. In the markets, this is precisely the time for *inaction*; sitting tight . . . ***or even buying more***

shares . . . during these panics can lead to handsome profits. Likewise, it is human nature to want to join with others in the good times, which means buying in ebullient and booming markets, usually near the top.

In response to the steadily rising stock markets of the decade, Federal Reserve chairman, Alan Greenspan, opined in 1997 that investors were driving the markets with "irrational exuberance" . . . and the markets responded with a short-lived decline followed by a big resurgence. The easily influenced investor panicked at the downturn and withdrew, missing the significant upturn that occurred before they rejoined the ride that continued for the next three years.

> Observation over many years has taught us that the chief losses to investors come from the purchase of low-quality securities at times of favorable business conditions.
> – Benjamin Graham
> Mentor of Warren Buffet

2. RECENCY. In everyday life, we tend to place a greater emphasis on our most recent experiences. These are the ones we think are most likely to recur in the future. We are never surprised when the weather forecast calls for tomorrow to be just like it was today. In the markets, this means that we expect trends to continue. The truth is that markets roll in long sine waves and seldom, if ever, in straight lines. Reversion to the mean almost guarantees that tomorrow is unpredictable, although investors believe they can simply extrapolate the recent trends.

3. OVER-RELIANCE ON DATA. We have become a datacentric society, leading us to assume a correlation always exists between the amount of data we have and the eventual outcome. Given enough data, we believe any problem is solvable. After all, it worked in the design of the space shuttle. Sufficient data make it possible to conduct successful heart transplants and minimize the chances of organ rejection. Studies and past experience have eliminated guesswork from the construction of bridges, buildings, and other infrastructure essential to modern society.

Virtually every aspect of our lives is improved with data . . . except investing in equities. The infamous "Dartboard Portfolios" published by *The Wall Street Journal* demonstrate that purely random selection of stocks often beats the best choices of experts.

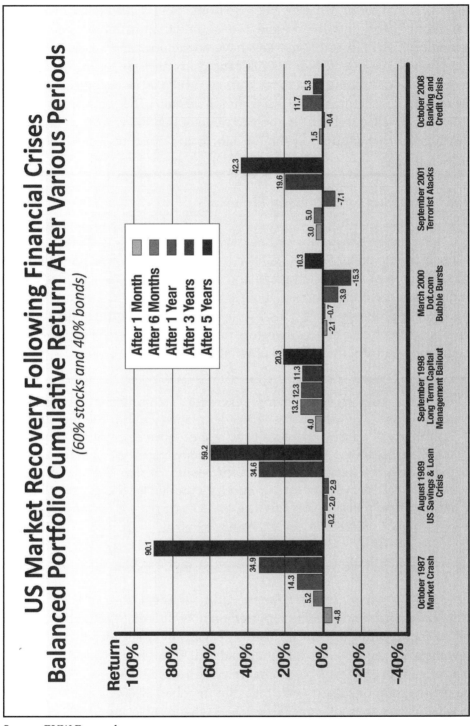

Source: RVW Research

Figure 10-1: Investors often fail to realize that events that have a temporary impact on the markets are frequently followed by sharp recoveries within five years.

4. *THE MYTH OF MEMORY*. Because human beings remember well and can recall history into the present, we assume that the markets, too, have a memory. The fact is that markets have no memory and no idea what we paid for an investment. Nor is it relevant to any decision we make or ought to make about holding or selling. Waiting until a stock or index returns to its original cost before selling is a common mistake. The best approach is to ask a very basic question: "If I owned none of that today, would I buy it?" The answer to that question should inform and direct the course of action to be followed.

The Development of Behavioral Economics

The earliest reference to behavioral economics is a 1979 paper by Daniel Kahneman and Amos Tversky, in which they observed that investors placed different weights on gains and losses. The researchers found that individuals are more worried about possible losses than they are excited by equally probable wins. This is often referred to as "prospect theory" and has proven that novice investors (and gamblers) perceive losing $1 as being more painful than the joy of winning $1.

> Of all the ways to invest money, ownership of profitable businesses has proved to be the optimal means of creating wealth. The rich do it; so can you. Indeed, investors have reaped greater profits by buying stock in corporate America than by lending out their money or by purchasing real estate and other hard assets. There is no reason to believe that stocks offer less opportunity today. In fact, you may have a tough time reaching your financial goals if you choose to avoid them.
>
> – Anne Farrelly
> *Invest Without Stress*

In their paper, *Prospect Theory: An Analysis of Decision Making Under Risk*, Kahneman and Tversky reported on how different groups responded when faced with different problems specifically associated with risk. In one instance, a group was told they had $1,000 and had to decide between a sure gain of $500 or a 50/50 chance of gaining $1,000 or nothing at all. Another group of subjects was told that they had $2,000, and their choice was between a sure loss of $500 or a 50/50 chance of losing $1,000 or losing nothing.

In the first group, 84% chose the sure gain. In the second group, only 31% opted for the certainty of a small loss. In mathematical terms, the two groups faced identical problems. The possible outcomes–ending up with $1,000 or $1,500 or $2,000–are exactly the same in each case. But the perception of certain gains has greater value to investors than certain losses.

In an entertaining application of this principle, MIT professor Dan Ariely writes about trick-or-treaters in his book, *Predictably Irrational: The Hidden Forces That Shape Our Decisions*. Ariely initially handed out three Hershey's Kisses to young children and then made them an offer. The kids could trade one piece of their chocolate for a miniature Snickers bar, or they could trade two of their Kisses for a full-size Snickers. Most children quickly handed over two small pieces of candy for the larger piece of candy. Later in the evening, the professor changed his terms and offered the large candy bar in exchange for all three Kisses or a bonus miniature candy bar for free.

Rationally, the trade maximized the amount of chocolate with which a child might end the evening. But, most children took the bonus bar and gave up nothing. In reality, they short-changed themselves by a factor of eight in terms of lost chocolate as the result of their decisions. Ariely thinks the driving factor in the decision-making process is "loss aversion" rather than gain maximization. He wrote, "There's no visible possibility of loss when we choose a free item (it's free)."

Meir Statman developed a concept known as *the fear of regret* which explains why investors often hang onto losers far too long. People often undergo a short period of remorse when they think they made an error in judgment. Statman theorized that sometimes investors avoid selling stocks showing a loss to avoid the pain of having to face the fact that they made a bad investment decision. This allows them to avoid the embarrassment of declaring the loss to the IRS, their accountant, and perhaps to their spouse.

> The masses. Them asses. Just move the "M" to see the crowds are always wrong.
> – Rip Van Winkle Wisdom

Other researchers believe that investors happily follow the crowd to avoid the feeling of regret when their decisions turn out to be wrong. It was common at the bursting of the Internet bubble in 2000-2001 to find investors taking solace in the fact that "everyone else owns it, so it is bound to come back soon," or, perhaps worse, finding comfort in the fact that they were not alone in their losses. The human brain has evolved to experience the pleasure of gain far less intensely than the pain of loss.

CONSIDER THESE TWO EXAMPLES OF LOSS AVERSION

1. *A HIGH PRICE MAKES A LOWER PRICE SEEM FAIR, EVEN WHEN IT'S NOT*

You're at a restaurant and the most expensive steak on the menu costs $50. But there's another one for $25. Choosing the $25 steak seems rational. You've considered the choices and made a decision heavily impacted by the existence of the $50 option. This phenomenon is referred to as "anchoring."

Anchoring is common on wine lists, says Richard Thaler, an economist at the University of Chicago Booth School of Business and co-author of *Nudge: Improving Decisions About Health, Wealth, and Happiness.* "Suppose the most expensive bottle on the list is $100 and nobody wants to buy it," he says. To boost sales of those $100 bottles, the restaurant adds a $200 bottle. "They could keep just one of them around. Nobody will order it."

Deciding which stock or fund to buy is frequently impacted by the relative prices of seemingly similar choices. However, every decision should be made independently and based on thorough research of that particular investment.

2. *FEAR OF LOSING MAKES UP FOR MISSING OUT ON WINNING MOVES*

Eric Johnson often conducts an experiment in his Columbia Business School class. He divides the class into two groups and asks one group how much they would pay for a mug. The typical response is $4. He gives the other group a mug for free, then asks, "How much would I have to pay you to part with it?" It's basically the same question: "How much is the mug worth to you?" Except this group gives an average response of $8.

Researchers call this the "endowment" effect. Johnson still finds it amazing–two randomly selected groups disagree dramatically over the value of a mug they hadn't seen moments before. "It's one of the most telling demonstrations in behavioral economics," he says. "Simply owning something increases its value."

Why? Because we really don't like losing something once we have it; as we have seen, the pain of losing outweighs the joy of winning. One consequence of *loss aversion*, says Thaler, is that we tend to prefer the "flat-rate" plans. We prefer to pay a fixed amount for monthly cell phone service, rather than being billed by the minute for our actual use. "Nobody likes to hear the meter running," he says.

Another finding of behavioral economics research is that people often strive to find order where none exists. Tversky worked with Thomas Gilovich to show that a basketball player, with what the fans consider a "hot hand," had the same chance of making his next shot as he did at any other time. Mathematically, they demonstrated that something which appears to be orderly, like a streak of consecutive shots in basketball, may very well be nothing more than good luck. Applying this lesson to mutual funds, a hot manager is no more likely to have a great year *next year* than he had in the previous year, yet investors have historically chased after the best performing funds with less than spectacular results.

In all walks of life, successful people have a great deal of confidence in their own abilities. But when it comes to investing, confidence has absolutely nothing to do with success. Confidence also impacts investment decisions in subtle ways. One published study demonstrated that investors have a tendency to invest in local companies, the ones with which they have the most familiarity and confidence in their future performance.

The study looked specifically at investors in telephone companies and found that they are more likely to own their local telephone company than one of the other, perhaps larger and more profitable, regional phone companies. No rational reason explained the geographic tendency associated with stock ownership. The authors attributed it solely to investor confidence in the company's future, grounded in their familiarity. This same tendency can afflict professionals and blind them to the changing circumstances decimating their favorite stocks.

> Investing is not a game where the guy with the 160 IQ beats the guy with the 130 IQ . . . once you have ordinary intelligence, what you need is the temperament to control the urges that get other people into trouble in investing.
>
> – Warren Buffett

Arnold S. Wood, of Martingale Asset Management, defines this as the "touchy-feely syndrome," explaining that people often overvalue things they've actually "touched" or personally selected. Proof for this concept is found in an academic experiment in which participants were either given a card or asked to select one from a stack. Those selecting their own cards were less likely to sell the card back to the researchers, eventually demanding up to four times as much as the price accepted by participants who were given theirs.

Researchers also believe that investment analysts who visit a company and meet with management develop excessive confidence in their opinion of the company, despite a lack of evidence to support this confidence. This argues further against individual stock selection.

Behavioral economics is one of those fascinating fields that impacts every aspect of life. For example, Richards J. Heuer, Jr. wrote an essay entitled "Do You Really Need More Information?" which was published in the book *Inside CIA's Private World: Declassified Articles from the Agency's Internal Journal 1955-1992.* Many may wonder what investors can learn from spies. Information overload is a very real problem within the intelligence community, and different sources often conflict with each other. The decision-making process an intelligence officer uses to sift through and analyze a mountain of data is very similar to the challenge faced by investors. Heuer studied professional handicappers–individuals who set betting odds at horse races. He found that the more information the handicappers were provided, the *worse* their accuracy. Interestingly, Heuer found that even though accuracy decreased, the handicappers' confidence in their forecasts doubled. His conclusion:

> Experienced analysts have an imperfect understanding of what information they actually use in making judgments. They are unaware of the extent to which their judgments are determined by a few dominant factors, rather than by the systematic integration of all available information. Analysts use much less available information than they think they do.

This is equally valid for investment analysts. Just as too much information lowers returns at the race track, it can also lower returns for investors.

"Bear Sterns is not in trouble," shouted Jim Cramer, the host of CNBC'S Mad Money, on March 11, 2008. "Don't move your money from Bear!" The Wall Street Bank collapsed just days later. As the financial crisis widened in the months that followed, Cramer made other similarly bad calls concerning Lehman Brothers and Bank of America.

In life, and in investing, we often think of our own decisions as rational while, at the same time, we question the ability of others to make sound decisions. Investors rely on information they think is better than the information on which most other investors are acting. In hindsight, they usually discover that the information was already factored into the stock price before they decided to act.

Each trade requires two sides–one person believing the stock will go up and another believing it will not. Only one will be correct, which highlights the difficulty of investment decisions. In a decision with a 50/50 chance of positive outcome, half of the choices will be wrong–only the seller or the buyer will have made the correct choice, not both.

There are many other studies that illustrate how thoughts and beliefs affect investment returns. The most important lesson for the individual investor is to remember that markets go through irrational phases. Remaining calm in times of excessive panic or "irrational exuberance," as Greenspan declared, and simply staying the course is the key to long-term profits. Being aware of your own tendency to make these mistakes is all that is required to avoid them.

> It is high time for broader industry acknowledgment that passive management is a preferable default for most individual investors, and that active management should come with a brighter warning sticker of sorts.
>
> –Tom Stabile, Writer
> *Financial Times*

The myriad complex studies may be distilled into this single, straightforward fact: *A simple strategy, such as buying and holding index-based ETFs, offers smart investors an opportunity to profit from the mistakes of the marketplace.*

For stock market investors, loss aversion impacts behavior profoundly. It causes most investors to hold losers too long and sell winners too early. When a stock tanks, we don't want to sell for a loss, so we hang on, hoping it will recover and avoid realizing the loss that has already been incurred.

BOND BUYERS BEWARE! Caveat Emptor!

Six things to watch out for when investing in bonds:

- **PRICING** Most brokers sell you bonds at marked-up prices, making an undisclosed profit on the sale. They act not as a broker but as a principal. (Instead you should buy bonds directly from a low-cost provider).

- **TIME HORIZON** Because bond prices and interest rates move inversely, long-term bonds work well in times of falling interest rates and poorly in times of appreciating rates. At times of relatively low interest rates, long-term bonds offer the likelihood of a severe decline in value as rates rise over time–and the further out you go, the greater this effect. [Suggestion: Use the laddered bond strategy which optimizes returns, stabilizes income and minimizes the losses from holding long-term bonds.]

- **SAFETY** Buying small issues or unrated ("junk") bonds presents numerous risks, including illiquidity and the loss of principal if the issuer defaults or goes bankrupt.

- **CALLABLE** Callable bonds are a "heads we win–tails you lose" proposition. If interest rates rise, bond prices will fall and you'll be stuck holding a poorly performing asset at a time when higher yields are available for similar bonds. On the other hand, if rates fall, bond prices will rise, and your bond will be probably be "called" (redeemed early) allowing the issuer to refinance at lower rates. You will end up replacing your relatively high interest income with bonds providing a lower return.

- **BOND FUNDS** Individual bonds have maturity dates, so even if rates move up and values decline, upon maturity the full face amount will ultimately be repaid. Bond funds, on other hand, usually have no maturity date and the loss may never be recovered.

- **ASSET ALLOCATION** The tendency to seek safety in bonds often misses the point that bonds, too, carry risks. Inflation ultimately impacts both the principal invested and the income.

Chapter 11
The Role of Bonds in a Portfolio

> I would say never do 100% of anything.
> — John C. Bogle

Bonds have their place in most portfolios, typically behaving in the opposite manner as stocks. Bonds also provide predictability of income and principal repayment. As you now know, stocks go through bear periods of undervaluation. Unsuitable for short-term investing, they tend to really shine over the longer term. Bonds, on the other hand, do quite nicely in the short-term, but inflation and the superior returns of equities over the long term tend to render bonds relatively poor performers by comparison. That's exactly why they work so well in combination.

Since bonds typically have lower long-term returns than stocks, investors often question why they need bonds in their portfolio at all. Three of the most compelling reasons are: bonds promise lower volatility in the portfolio, they provide a predictable stream of income and principal repayment, and they may offer tax advantages.

It is widely believed that bonds are less volatile than stocks. This is generally true over the long term, but it is not always true when looking at shorter holding periods. There are times when bonds experience significantly greater short-term volatility than do stocks. Over the long term, government bonds may experience half as much volatility compared to the major stock indexes. However, the annualized standard deviation of bonds is about 10%, which means you can lose a significant amount of money in any given year. In fact, bond owners actually lose money in one out of every five years, on average.

Portfolio stability is an important, but often overlooked, investment objective. As part of a portfolio, bonds act as a buffer against the volatility of stocks, while stocks dampen the volatility of bonds. This synergy increases the consistency of total portfolio returns. Statistically, holding a combination of stocks and bonds has the potential to generate returns close to those seen in a stocks-only investment strategy while, at the same time, substantially lowering the risk of being fully invested.

Bonds are also important to ensure that you have access to cash when you need it. An investor with an all-stock portfolio may find himself in the midst of a bear market when money is needed to pay that long-anticipated college tuition bill. If you were forced to liquidate stocks at that time, you would endure all the pain associated with realized market losses and necessarily miss the gains that inevitably follow when the uptrend in equities resumes. Bond investments, however, may be timed, or "laddered," according to their redemption dates to provide cash when required and to limit the downside while waiting for that day to arrive.

Because they pay interest on a regular schedule, bonds offer investors consistent income. A bond is a contract between a company and a borrower to pay interest to the owner of the bond at scheduled times and return the principal on a definite date. This differs from stocks whose dividends are subject to change, and may even be discontinued at any time by the company's board of directors based upon current business conditions. Even if a company were to skip a bond interest payment, they are still legally obligated to make it up in the future.

> Fund Giants Take Competing Stands on Bond Outlook: Pimco's Bill Gross has been selling Treasurys. BlackRock's Rick Rieder has been buying.
> — *The Wall Street Journal*
> April 24, 2011

High-income investors often consider bonds as a way to provide tax-free income. Payments from most municipal bonds are exempt from federal income taxes and often enjoy a respite from state income taxes as well. Municipal bonds are issued by states, cities, or other local government agencies to pay for infrastructure improvements or general operating expenses. They are often referred to as "munis." Although they may offer a lower interest rate than corporate bonds, their tax advantage makes them highly competitive investments.

As has been stated, no investment is without risk, and although bonds are thought of as being safe, there are some very important risk factors to be aware of. As long you hold it, the price of that bond will fluctuate, sometimes on a daily basis. When held to maturity, the full nominal (par) value will be repaid.

Interest rates change frequently, and these changes are too difficult to predict. Bond prices are inversely related to changes in interest rates; when rates increase, the prices of the bonds you are holding will decrease, and vice versa.

The interest rate on a bond is defined at the time the bond is first offered for sale. This interest rate, known as the *coupon*, will be based on interest rates in the general economy at the time the bond is issued. Over time, market rates change, but the coupon does not. If interest rates move higher, investors may not be willing to buy the bonds at face (or par) value. For example, if an investor buys a bond with a 4% coupon and interest rates rise to 5%, new issues will have to pay 5% and no one would be likely to buy a 4% bond at its par value.

To help ensure there is someone willing to buy the bond, the market revalues the price of the 4% bond lower ("at a discount" from $1,000) so that the eventual repayment of principal, together with the interest payments over time, will offset the lower coupon rate. This should not matter to an investor holding the bond to maturity, since the principal will be repaid in full at that time (unless you also purchased the bond at a "premium,"–an amount greater than $1,000–in which case the "yield to maturity" will be even lower).

Occasionally, companies go out of business or go into bankruptcy. This is a risk that bond or stock holders face with any of their holdings. If this happens, the value of your bond can fall to zero. Only US Treasury bonds are completely free of this "default risk" because it is generally believed that the government will simply print more money if it needs to (if it cannot sell more bonds to finance the redemption of existing bonds).

> If, for example, you plan to leave most of your capital in bequests to your children, the appropriate time horizon for your family investment policy-even if you are well into your seventies or eighties-may well be so long-term that you'd be correct to ignore such investment conventions as the canard, "older people should invest in bonds for higher income and greater safety."
>
> – Charles Ellis, Author
> *Timeless Strategies for Successful Investing*

Current interest rates dictate the coupon rate the bond issuer must set for any given series of bonds, and default risk is factored in. The greater the default risk, the higher the coupon rate. With government bonds or high-quality corporate bonds, there is less risk that an interest payment will be skipped or the principal will not be repaid, and their coupon rates are among the lowest. "Junk" bonds, on the other end of the spectrum, are those considered less than investment grade. They carry more risk of default, and loss of principal coupled with missed interest payments is a very real possibility. For this reason, junk bonds are forced to pay higher interest rates.

Another factor that influences bond interest rates is the prospect of inflation. Inflation eats away at the purchasing power of your periodic interest payments and also means the principal will be worth less when it is eventually repaid. If there were concerns about future inflation, bond interest rates will be higher to compensate investors for this increased risk and to attract their money.

Bonds also have a unique risk factor known as *reinvestment risk.* Just as it is impossible to predict the stock market, it is impossible to reliably predict general interest rates in the economy. In the early 1980s, long-term US Treasury bonds offered double digit yields, because inflation had been running rampant for nearly a decade. By the time these bonds were fully repaid, inflation was under control–almost non-existent through most of the 1990s–and there were no new low-risk alternatives available to investors offering this high level of income. Reinvestment risk means an investor may suffer a real drop in current income if unable to obtain the same rate in the future economic environment.

Although the media and the average investor pay far more attention to stocks, bonds represent an equally important component of a well-diversified investment portfolio. By reducing volatility, they add safety for the prudent investor. Steady income from interest payments greatly improves one's ability to plan for long-term goals. The tax advantages certain bonds afford may help you keep more of your income and must not be overlooked. Bonds, used smartly and with an understanding of the hazards, are a definite complement to equities.

Chapter 12
The 5-Year Laddered Bond Portfolio:
A Systematic Approach to
Maximizing Income and Minimizing Risk

> Fixed income investors have been paralyzed by the fear of rising interest rates. Many investors have elected to hold cash rather than to reinvest farther out on the yield curve in maturities that offer higher interest rates.
>
> – Ed Easterling
> Crestmont Research

Bonds come in many flavors: taxable or tax-free, Treasury, investment-grade, high-yield, junk, and more. For affluent investors, holding individual bonds is usually preferable to bond funds; however, selecting individual bonds requires more effort than choosing an index-ETF.

Fear is a common problem among investors. Fear of missing out on stock market gains prevents some investors from holding fixed income assets. Fear that rates will rise causes some investors to delay committing to fixed income investments. Other fears factor into the asset allocation process, and all can be addressed with a relatively simple strategy.

Taxable vs. Tax-free Bonds

The "best" method of investing in bonds necessarily varies from one individual investor to another. The first question to address is in relation to taxes. Income-tax-free municipal bonds are usually attractive to investors in the upper income tax brackets. While the interest rate is lower, the after-tax return may be greater, depending on the market rates available. To do an "apples-to-apples" comparison, you first need to determine what a taxable bond's interest rate is on an after-tax basis in order to compare it with the tax-free bond's interest rate. The larger value identifies which bond truly provides more income and represents the best investment.

Determining the equivalent after-tax rate starts with knowing your marginal income tax rate, including federal, state, and local income taxes. If you are in the 28% federal bracket, with state taxes of 9%, and local taxes of 3%, your marginal tax rate is around 37%.[1] That value is used in the following formula:

$$\text{Equivalent taxable yield} = \frac{100 * \text{tax-free yield}}{100 - \text{marginal tax rate}}$$

So, if you were evaluating a municipal bond with a 4% coupon, the formula would tell us that an equivalent taxable yield is about 6.35%:

$$\text{Equivalent taxable yield} = \frac{100 * 0.04}{100 - 0.37} = 6.35\%$$

Thus, if we can find a taxable bond with a yield of more than 6.35%, coupled with the degree of safety we are seeking, it would provide more after-tax income than the 4% municipal bond would provide income-tax-free and would be the better income-producing choice.

Considering money held in a taxable account, most individuals in higher income tax brackets will derive a greater benefit by owning tax-free municipal bonds. It is inappropriate, however, to hold any tax-free bonds in a qualified retirement account (e.g., Keogh, SEP, 401(k), 403(b), IRA/Roth IRA), because one's otherwise tax-free interest will be taxed upon withdrawal, defeating the tax-free advantage and actually resulting in a loss of potential income.

The issue of taxes is never straightforward, and the Alternative Minimum Tax (AMT) often impacts unwary municipal bond holders. The AMT may cause the interest from certain municipal bonds–especially those used to fund airports and industrial projects–to be counted as income for some taxpayers, negating the value of the tax-free bonds. A detailed understanding of the specifics of the AMT usually requires the assistance of both your accountant and investment advisor.

When purchasing individual bonds, taxable munis can be avoided. However, municipal bond mutual funds and ETFs may hold these bonds, which means they will regularly distribute income subject to the AMT to their shareholders. Although municipal bonds with an exposure to AMT frequently offer slightly higher interest rates than other munis, it is rarely enough to offset the actual tax liability. And while mutual funds or ETFs are ideal investment choices for the stock portion of your portfolio, individually purchased bonds often represent a better investment than owning shares of bond funds because bond mutual funds have no set maturity date.

How the Bond Ladder Works

One strategy for the fixed income portion of your portfolio is known as a bond *ladder*. The goal of the ladder is to ensure a more stable, long-term rate of return. The advantage of the ladder is that it lowers the risks associated with long-term, fixed-income investments.

All bonds have maturity dates–the date on which the bond is redeemed and the principal is repaid. If all bond investments matured on the same date, then you would be forced to reinvest at whatever interest rate the market was offering at that time. After an original bond purchase, if interest rates decline, when a bond is eventually redeemed, the principal will either earn less income going forward or an investor will have to purchase bonds with inherently greater risk in their pursuit of additional, fixed income. This is known as *reinvestment risk*, and is associated with all fixed-income investments such as bonds and bank CDs.

Laddering, on the other hand, involves buying bonds with differing maturities. Short-term bonds have less volatility but tend to offer lower interest rates than long-term bonds. But increasing income by investing only in long-term bonds will expose you to wide fluctuations in price during your holding period as general interest rates rise or fall, creating additional potential for loss if you are forced to sell before the maturity date. Properly executed, bond laddering mitigates some of the risk in the inevitable swings in interest rates.

1900-2010	BOND LADDERS		
	5-YEAR	10-YEAR	20-YEAR
AVERAGE RETURN	4.6%	4.8%	4.9%
MINIMUM RETURN	0.4%	0.2%	-2.1%
MAXIMUM RETURN	15.5%	16.2%	21.0%

Source: Crestmont Research

Table 12-1: Five-year bond ladders have provided consistent returns with less volatility compared to longer-term bond ladders.

To build a laddered portfolio, it is necessary to buy an assortment of bonds with maturities distributed over a given period of time. For example, to construct a five-year ladder, you would invest equal amounts in bonds maturing at one-, two-, three-, four-, and five-year intervals. When the first bonds mature, the principal would be reinvested in a new bond with a five-year maturity, maintaining the time-to-maturity structure of the ladder.

With a five-year bond ladder, the average investment period is two-and-one-half years, but once the program is in place, you will always be reinvesting in new five-year bonds which tend to pay higher rates than bonds with shorter maturities.

Furthermore, because one-fifth of the portfolio is maturing each year, you would have a regular source of liquidity if needed. Risk is significantly less than for an investor who owned only long-term bonds, and there is better insulation against erratic interest rate swings.

If interest rates do decline, you will have to reinvest the principal being repaid at a lower rate, but you will continue to benefit from the above-market return offered by the other issues in your ladder. As interest rates rise, your total portfolio will quickly catch up as reinvestments each year acquire new bonds paying higher rates. This strategy mitigates reinvestment risk because your money is being reinvested throughout an interest rate cycle, and your portfolio actually provides returns closer to those of the longer term bonds . . . *but with substantially less risk.*

Over more than a century, five-year bond ladders have never had a losing year. Since 1900, this strategy has delivered an average return of 4.6% per year, only fractionally less than ladders of longer duration. The consistency of returns for the five-year ladder makes this an ideal strategy for almost all investors.

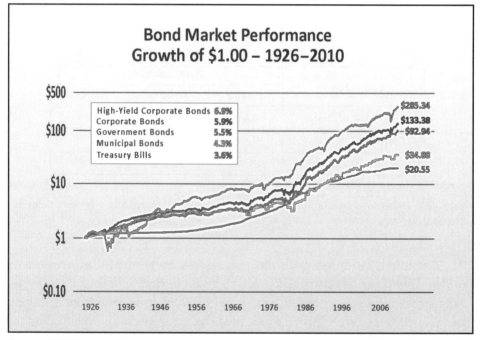

Source: RVW Research

Figure 12-1: Although bond returns generally move in the same direction, the various types of bonds provide real returns according to their risk profile.

The basics of laddered bond investing are relatively simple: purchase, redeem, replace. It is a classic, time-tested strategy that both requires discipline and reduces speculation. The initial implementation of this strategy is a bit more complex than buying and holding equity ETFs, but once in place, the only action required is spending–or investing–the annual interest income and reinvesting the principal each year as a portion of the portfolio matures.

One additional hazard of bond investing concerns those issues which are "callable." The issuer hedges its debt position by selling bonds that may be redeemed earlier than their stated maturity. In the event interest rates fall, the issuer may be able to borrow at more favorable rates. Rather than pay higher interest on existing debt, they may sell new, lower-yielding bonds to provide funds necessary to repurchase older debt. Although an investor will not lose any principal in such a transaction, he will lose the stream of current income the bond was providing and will be unlikely to replace it with other similarly rated bonds that provide the same level of income. This is known as *call risk*, and it can be avoided only by not purchasing bonds that have an early call provision.

Callable bonds may initially be discounted (sold for less than the par value) or offer a slightly higher interest rate to attract investors and to help offset the risk. An investor seeking to replace a bond called within a particular ladder may discover that he must pay a premium (more than the par value) for a replacement bond because it will pay a higher rate of interest than new issues are paying. The bond will eventually be redeemed for its $1,000 par value, but inflation will have eroded the purchasing power of that $1,000. Conversely, if interest rates rise, the investor will find himself holding a bond for which there may be no willing purchasers, since new bonds are available that pay a higher rate of return–unless the purchase price is deeply discounted. This is *liquidity risk*.

For this reason, we refer to callable bonds as a "heads we win–tails you lose" proposition. There is nothing an investor can do to protect against call risk if exposed to it. As with all bonds, if interest rates rise, you'll be stuck with a poorly performing but income-producing asset. New bonds will be issued paying those higher rates, yours will decline in trading value to maintain its yield to maturity, and you will suffer *inflation risk*. But if interest rates decline, the issuer will call the bond and refinance its debt at the new, lower rates. In a changing interest rate environment–up or down–*you cannot win* when a bond is called.

---

[1] Combined marginal tax rates are affected by each investor's deductibilty of state and local taxes on their federal tax return, as well as by the availability of miscellaneous deductions.

Chapter 13
The Agony and the Ecstasy
of Hedge Fund Investing

Investing in a hedge fund is the ultimate act of blind faith.
– Rip Van Winkle Wisdom

Lifting the Veil

Anyone who reads *The Wall Street Journal* will have an acute awareness of the popularity and infamy of hedge funds, the ubiquitous, yet somewhat obscure, investment vehicles that are known for producing earth-shattering returns on one hand and catastrophic blow-ups on the other. One need only say the words "Madoff" or "Amaranth Advisors" to conjure up fear and dread among those who invest in hedge funds. Amaranth Advisors was a hedge fund with about $9 billion under management. In September 2006, it suffered a spectacular collapse as it lost nearly $6 billion in one week. The manager had made a large–and incorrect–bet on natural gas futures.

Ultimately, hedge funds are poorly understood by and inappropriate for most investors. Even those investors, who have the appetite for risk, and the means and sophistication to play in this space, need to be well-armed with the facts. It is true that hedge funds can provide attractive returns if the best performers are chosen. However, given the risks and the fact that a hedge fund is basically a non-transparent and unregulated investment, this category should occupy only a very small place, if any, in a Rip Van Winkle portfolio.

Hedge funds are private investment partnerships that employ a variety of sophisticated strategies in an attempt to provide strong returns while remaining uncorrelated to the stock market. While today many consider it a risky asset class, hedge funds originally started as vehicles designed to reduce risk. In 1945, Alfred W. Jones, a financial journalist, devised an innovative strategy for protecting his investors from downside risk. Jones bought stocks he thought were undervalued and then he "hedged" his bet by selling borrowed shares (selling "short") of those stocks that he thought were over-valued.

Jones' strategy was based on the belief that if the market went up, his "long" positions (shares he owned) would increase in value. On the other hand, if the markets had a downturn, his "short" positions would increase in value, offsetting any losses to his "long" positions. While this strategy, known as *long/short*, is still in use by many hedge funds today, the term "hedge fund" has come to refer more to a particular structure of investment rather than a particular strategy.

In fact, hedge funds today employ myriad strategies and are often classified into categories such as capital arbitrage, distressed debt, event-driven, multi-strategy, and several others. Each of these funds tends to employ strategies far more sophisticated than most veteran investors could use on their own. They often trade in rather esoteric securities such as derivatives, futures contracts, synthetics, and convertibles. Some hedge funds, known as *quant funds,* build sophisticated computer models in order to identify mispriced securities and buy or sell large amounts of stock to profit from perceived momentary mispricing by the markets.

> It's only when the tide goes out that you can see who was swimming without shorts.
> – Warren Buffett

Gee, I'm Sorry Your Hedge Fund Blew Up

Unlike their historical origins, modern-day hedge funds often focus less on mitigating risk and more on maximizing returns. As a result, these funds may use a significant amount of leverage. They purchase securities with borrowed money, resulting in both amplified gains and losses. This, combined with the opaque nature of these investments, makes it extremely difficult for investors to know exactly how much risk they are taking.

Part of what makes assessing the risk so difficult is the very structure of the funds and the nature of their activities. Since these investment vehicles are usually organized as partnerships, they may not be required to register with the SEC or disclose their activities to third parties, including their own investors. Hedge funds are only lightly regulated compared to other investments, like mutual funds, partly because their investors must be *accredited,* meaning they have a net worth of at least $1 million (as an individual) or meet some other greater minimum financial criteria.

Another restriction is that the number of investors in a hedge fund is limited, and very high minimum investments (some established funds require $1 million or more) may be required. The government-mandated limitations are intended to limit participation in hedge funds to highly sophisticated individuals who understand the risk and can afford to lose all of their investment. Tightened investor qualifications are currently being considered by the SEC.

A commonly overlooked risk factor is that many hedge funds invest in relatively illiquid assets, including derivatives and financial instruments that are difficult to understand. Because it is so difficult for the manager to quickly exit from these positions, they need to make it difficult for their own investors to access their money. Withdrawals from hedge funds are usually allowed only a few times a year, rarely more often than quarterly, and sometimes those withdrawal terms can be unilaterally modified by the manager.

Because they tend to trade in securities that are seldom bought or sold, hedge fund managers need to keep their positions as secret as possible. If others found out what they owned, astute traders could develop strategies designed to take advantage of the problems associated with illiquidity. Mutual funds report everything they own at least twice a year, while hedge funds may never have to report their holdings. This lack of transparency involves great risks, and, in fact, many hedge funds have imploded with devastating consequences for their investors.

Anybody who has ever purchased a lottery ticket understands the first basic rule of investing: the greater the risk of loss, the greater the return and *vice versa*. The person buying a lottery ticket knows that the odds of winning are overwhelmingly against him, but because the prize is so incredibly large, he is willing to place a small bet in hopes of winning the jackpot. The vast majority lose that bet. The risk is large, but so is the potential reward, and the pursuit of the reward overshadows the risk.

> People think I am a gambler. I've never gambled in my life. To me, a gambler is someone who plays slot machines. I prefer to own slot machines.
> – Donald J. Trump

The difference between a professional gambler and an amateur is not that the professional avoids all risk, since doing so would eliminate all reward. Rather, he will place only those bets where he believes he is taking the smallest possible risk in order to get the greatest rewards in the exchange. A hedge fund manager is employing all of his sophisticated strategies to do essentially the same thing.

Sometimes, however, the allure of striking it rich results in unintended consequences. Moreover, sometimes the risk being taken is not fully understood. Amaranth Advisors' spectacular fall from grace, in which star energy trader Brian Hunter's aggressive bets resulted in a loss of $6 billion–65% of the firm's total assets–in one week, is epic. In 2005, Hunter had made incredible profits buying derivatives that increased in value as the price of natural gas rose. Along came Hurricane Katrina, and Hunter looked like a genius. He made the same prediction the next year, but without a major hurricane, the price of natural gas plummeted and so did the hedge fund. The staggering loss forced the fund out of business.

> We have a higher percentage of the intelligentsia engaged in buying and selling pieces of paper. A great civilization will bear a lot of abuse, but there are dangers in the current situation that threaten anyone who swings for the fences.
>
> – Charlie Munger, Vice Chairman
> Berkshire Hathaway, Inc.

Unfortunately, for many hedge fund investors, the Amaranth disaster was not an isolated occurrence. Rather, there have been a spate of funds with breathtaking draw downs over the last several years. Even funds run by Wall Street giants, such as Citibank and Goldman Sachs, have suffered losses of billions of dollars. The fraudulent Ponzi scheme operated by Bernie Madoff, for more than thirty years some suspect, is another example of how the allure of unending gains can blind investors to the realities of the stock markets. Madoff's "funds" managed to provide positive "returns" in the 5%–8% range in 2008, at the same time that the US stock markets were experiencing a *negative* 33%–38% downturn.

The red flags were ignored for years by investors and regulators alike. This was, after all, Bernie Madoff. By his own admission following his arrest in late 2008, Madoff had stopped investing any of the money being funneled to his firm as early as the mid-1990's. It's entirely possible that he never invested a penny of it at all. Despite court-ordered restitution to his victims amounting to more than $170 billion, Madoff has steadfastly remained silent concerning the whereabouts of his funds' assets.

Perhaps the most famous example of a hedge fund gone bad was Long-Term Capital Management, founded by two Nobel Prize-winning and very successful Wall Street traders. This hedge fund was considered to be the best investment in the world, one that virtually assured investors of outstanding performance in any market environment. Initially, the fund nearly tripled the money of its wealthy investors between its inception in March 1994 and the end of 1997. Its sophisticated trading strategy was described as "market-neutral-engineered"–meaning it had the ability to make money whether underlying bond prices were rising or falling.

For some reason, the markets stopped doing what they were supposed to do in August 1998, and Long-Term Capital suffered a 44% loss in a single month. At the time, Chief Executive John W. Meriwether, a legendary bond trader, understated the pain of his investors when he said, "August has been very painful for all of us." By October of that year, the fund had lost more than $4.6 billion and the Federal Reserve was forced to intervene in order to preserve the integrity of the global financial system.

Amazingly, this step toward the edge of a worldwide financial collapse did little to slow the growth of hedge funds or discourage investors from joining in. Investors have continued to buy these funds, and there are now thousands of hedge funds controlling trillions of dollars. Hedge fund managers are also rewarded much more handsomely than most mutual fund managers. Due to the limited regulation and lax disclosure requirements, exact statistics on hedge funds are difficult to obtain. However, according to Hedge Fund Research Inc., assets under management of the hedge fund industry totaled $2.6 trillion at the end of 2010.

Fees, Fees, and More Fees

If hedge funds are so dangerous, why have they proliferated to such an extent? In order to answer this question, one needs to understand the reasons why hedge funds are created and how they raised capital for these funds.

For anybody with the perceived skill and the relationships necessary to open up a hedge fund, the rationale for doing so is clear. Hedge fund managers often receive fees from 1%–3% of assets under management and as much as an additional 20% of profits, known as *carried interest*. That means that a manager who is managing a $100 million fund with a typical 2% fee takes home $2 million . . . *even if his fund is losing money*. If his fund's value is up 10% for the year, he pockets an additional $2 million. By simply matching the 10% long-term compounding rate of the market, he takes home $4 million while his investors end up with a 6% net return. In fact, for many managers, their very *raison d'être* is to raise as much capital as possible, since merely increasing total assets under management is often an easier way to generate fee income than attempting to beat the market and achieving actual capital appreciation for the investors.

Given the math, it's a wonder that these managers are successful in raising the capital at all. Managers who cannot show a track record of attractive net after-fee returns will not be successful in attracting large amounts of capital. That being said, there is an entire business built around introducing capital to these managers. Often times a capital introducer will take 15%-25% of the manager's profits in proportion to the capital he introduces. This reality creates a situation in which there is no shortage of willing salesmen looking to push the latest fund.

> If your hedge fund went up 300% one year and lost 90% the next year, you are not up a net 210%. Nor is it relevant to consider that the average annual increase is 105%.
>
> – Rip Van Winkle Wisdom

Also, much of the money deployed into hedge funds belongs to large institutions that need to put their money to work profitably. They also sometimes do additional business with the managers or have special fee arrangements that provide better terms than other (smaller) investors. For all these reasons, Wall Street has a vested interest in continuing to bolster the hedge fund industry.

Do Hedge Funds Ever Make Sense?

Up to this point, the discussion has primarily focused on the unseen perils of hedge fund investing. For the average conservative investor, it should be persuasive enough for them to simply stay away.

On the other hand, there are many investors who can afford to take large risks and would be willing to take such chances in order to enhance their capital appreciation beyond the 10% long-term compounding rate of index funds. For such an individual simply looking at the high double- and even triple-digit returns, some of the top-performing hedge funds appear to make a compelling case.

Moreover, as a class, they often can and will outperform market indexes. Demonstrating this conclusively is difficult, because the secretive nature of many funds makes data collection difficult. That being said, there are several companies tracking hedge fund performance and constructing indexes based on the publicly available data.

For example, according to Hedgefund.net, the HFN Aggregate index of 4,221 hedge funds returned 10.56% in 2010. The MCSI Hedge Fund Composite (All World) index earned 10.62%. The S&P 500® Total Return Index was 15.06% for 2010 (including reinvested dividends), and the Dow Jones 30 Industrials gained 11.02%. But the HFN Short Bias Index managed to *lose* 15.25% in an otherwise winning year across all other HFN indexes.

In all, 2010 was a respectable, if not lackluster, year for most hedge funds compared to other indexes. In years past, hedge funds have provided investors with both superior returns and spectacular losses. The very wide spread between best and worst performers in the same year reveals the great risks involved in selecting a hedge fund in which to invest.

Perhaps the most serious problem that hedge funds present to the investor is the fact that they tend to involve an extremely active portfolio management style. Any gains made will tend to be taxed in the year earned at the higher income tax rates which could approach 45% for those living in states where there is also a high income tax. These investments are therefore extremely tax-inefficient because they generate huge short-term capital gains that are subject to ordinary income tax rates.

> If you lie on the floor with your feet in a freezer and your head in a furnace, on average, you would be feeling comfortable. The fact that, on average, hedge funds have delivered satisfactory returns is of no comfort to all those who saw theirs evaporate.
>
> – Rip Van Winkle Wisdom

Comparing the hedge fund indexes to the stock markets is also difficult over the long run, as there are not sufficient historical data to determine long-term returns. Moreover, when each of these indexes is broken down according to strategy, the returns will diverge over any given time period.

It's hard to argue against what appears to be some very tempting returns. According to Morningstar, the top performing hedge fund they tracked in 2007 gained 869.56%; there were three other funds whose returns were over 200%, and seventeen funds had net returns exceeding 100%. In all, each of the top one hundred funds tracked gained more than 50% for the year. However, 2008 was a nightmare year for investors, with hedge funds losing more than 18% (but this was only half the 37% loss in the S&P 500® Index).

The challenge with hedge fund investing is that in order to have average returns even close to broad market indexes, there have to be many complete losers to offset the big winners. Once you decide that you want to be in the game, how do you decide which game to play? Institutional investors adhere to extensive due diligence processes and still fall prey to catastrophic implosions. Individual investors cannot be expected to fare any better. Style rotation and natural market cycles tend to make the search for the best funds extremely challenging.

Another difficulty with these funds is that many of the superior performers tend to be closed to new investors. Once a manager feels his strategy can no longer be utilized with a larger capital base, he will either close his fund to new money or severely limit who can come in. Closing a fund also adds to its mystique and makes it more popular. Unless the investor has the right relationships (or "connections"), he is unlikely to have access to the best funds.

Funds of Funds

One way that investors get around the daunting challenges of hedge fund selection and accessibility limitations imposed by the best funds is through investing in funds of funds (FOFs) that hold interests in other hedge funds as their primary asset class. These funds will seek exposure to a multiplicity of managers, strategies, and styles. Sometimes these funds will employ leverage, at the fund level, in an attempt to enhance returns, albeit with an additional measure of risk.

Generally speaking, FOF investors are willing to pay an additional layer of fees for the manager to spend the time researching and conducting due diligence on the underlying funds. FOFs can also provide market-beating returns, while diversifying away the catastrophic risk of any particular fund. As such, their returns will rarely come close to their single-fund counterparts. The 2010 aggregate average returns of the FOFs was a mere 5% compared to the 10.56% average of all hedge funds.

> Buy low-cost index funds, which will outperform the majority of other investors (the vast majority), and avoid hedge funds.
> – Warren Buffett

Looking at all the data on hedge funds, an investor may feel the compulsion to take part in what seems to be a market-beating opportunity. He may even be compelled by analysts' arguments that many hedge funds do not move in lock step with broader market indexes. This lack of correlation may even appear to make a case for including some hedge fund holdings in one's portfolio seem reasonable to certain investors.

Even so, the risks inherent in hedge funds generally make them inappropriate as core holdings for any individual investor. Rather, they should be held as "satellite" investments that will augment and supplement a core broad market portfolio. Moreover, with the advent of new "investable" indexes, any investor can, theoretically, include a hedge fund index in his portfolio of index funds and sleep well knowing that so long as the hedge fund party continues, he will not be leaving alone.

Chapter 14
Dollar-Cost Averaging:
Diversifying Over Time

> Now is always the most difficult time to invest.
> — Rip Van Winkle Wisdom

It is important to have a plan for a gradual entry into the market and an exit strategy designed to meet your life needs while accepting the fact that markets can decline sharply and suddenly. The decision on when to buy *or* sell is different than the decisions about whether to buy *and* when to sell. Understanding this distinction is important for successful investors.

Dollar-cost averaging is a well-known investment technique. It is usually thought of as investing a fixed amount into stocks, bonds, ETFs, or mutual funds every month. This idea protects you from using all of your investment capital to buy something at the market peak and watching your investment value plummet into the trough. It is a very effective strategy for reducing timing risk, since the price of each purchase will be very likely to fluctuate and the impact of market volatility is lessened.

This "get rich slowly" strategy is the basis of most retirement plans. Each month, the employee contributes a small part of his salary to fund the prospect of a brighter future. Over time, these small amounts grow to a sizable account. Most people make the strategic decision to invest a large portion of their retirement accounts into equities. Using a tax-advantaged account, the tactical decision of when to buy is dictated largely by their employer and the tax laws. Buying a small amount on each payday avoids the decision of whether the market is high or low. Annual contribution limits also help investors to sidestep the timing decision. Timing the investment this way is one of the best things you can do to passively take advantage of an upward trend in the markets, while occasionally buying more during periods of market decline.

Diversification among the holdings in one's portfolio is another common investment technique; properly used, it can limit the overall risk and volatility. Dollar-cost averaging is a form of diversification over time, an idea that introduces a different type of risk-reducing diversification to the portfolio. Instead of investing all of your assets as a single lump sum at one time, you work into the position by slowly buying smaller amounts over a longer period of time. This spreads your cost basis over several periods, insulating you somewhat from the risk of a sharp change in market prices.

To see the value of dollar-cost averaging in action, consider the hypothetical investor suffering from *"irrational exuberance"* in April 2000 with $500,000 to invest. Investing the entire sum into an ETF that tracks the S&P 500®, this investor would have lost nearly 20% of that investment only five years later. However, by investing $62,500 once every three months over the next eight quarters instead, the loss would have been minimized to just 7% (mostly in the price of one's shares), an amount that would have been almost completely offset by dividends received and reinvested.

> I had never managed money. I had never made any real money ... yet I was holding myself out as a great expert on matters of finance. I was telling people what to do with millions of dollars when the largest financial complication I had ever encountered was a $325 overdraft in my account at the Chase Manhattan Bank.
>
> – Michael Lewis, Author
> *Liar's Poker*

A variation of this concept is dollar-*value* averaging, a technique that increases the portfolio value by a set amount each period. While dollar-cost averaging requires investing a fixed amount of money during each time period, dollar value averaging requires the portfolio value to grow by a set amount each time period. Although this technique may be too complex (or costly) for most investors, high-net-worth individuals might consider dollar-value averaging as a way to meet long-term capital appreciation goals.

To apply this strategy, when the market declines, you will need to add more to your account; in bull markets, however, you contribute less ... and might even need to *withdraw* some funds in any given time period. It takes full advantage of the "buy low, sell high" concept that many investors fail to achieve. The investor is continually rebalancing his portfolio.

Proponents of dollar-value averaging point out that this method guarantees a return on your investment. The downside to this strategy is that you may have to supply a large amount of cash if the market experiences a significant decline. However, research has demonstrated that the method will result in higher returns with about the same amount of risk as dollar cost averaging, especially over long time horizons.

An Example of Dollar-Cost Averaging

MONTH	AMOUNT INVESTED	PRICE PER SHARE	SHARES PURCHASED
1	$1,000	$200.00	5.00
2	$1,000	$100.00	10.00
3	$1,000	$50.00	20.00
4	$1,000	$300.00	3.33
5	$1,000	$500.00	2.00
6	$1,000	$400.00	2.50
TOTALS / AVERAGES	$6,000 / 6 = $1,000	$1,550 / 6 = $258.33	42.83 SHARES @ $140.09/SHARE

Table 14-1: Systematically investing the same amount each month reduces the cost of acquiring shares by taking advantage of price declines and reducing the number of shares purchased when prices are high. As shown, the investor purchases shares at an average cost per share 45.7% less than the average price per share.

An Example of Share-Cost Averaging

MONTH	SHARES PURCHASED	PRICE PER SHARE	TOTAL INVESMENT
1	20	$200.00	$4,000.00
2	20	$100.00	$2,000.00
3	20	$50.00	$1,000.00
4	20	$300.00	$6,000.00
5	20	$500.00	$10,000.00
6	20	$400.00	$8,000.00
TOTALS / AVERAGES	20 * 6 = 120 SHARES	$1,550/6 = $258.33	$31,000 / 6 = $5,166.67/MONTH

Table 14-2: Purchasing a fixed number of shares each month requires a larger investment when share prices are high and results in the higher average price per share compared to dollar-cost averaging. The difference, however, is that using the dollar-cost averaging method and investing the same $5,166.67 each month would result in the acquisition of 221.30 shares . . . 84.4% more shares with the same $31,000.

It might be said that dollar-cost averaging is like putting $20 worth of gasoline in your tank every time you pull into the gas station. When the price of gasoline is high, you buy fewer gallons, and when the price is low you buy more. On the other hand, dollar-value averaging is like filling up the tank every time you need gas. Some days you'll pay more, and some days you'll pay less, but you will always leave the station with a full tank of gas. You could discover that filling your tank once a week compared to buying $20 worth of gasoline every other day actually saves a little money over the same time period as the price of gasoline fluctuates a few pennies per gallon.

An Entry and Exit Strategy

While dollar-cost averaging is usually thought of as a way to enter the market, it is equally effective as an exit strategy. Given the long-term upward trend of the market, it makes sense to sell a little at a time rather than all at once.

Large investors typically employ this strategy. Bill Gates is believed to sell an average of $20 million worth of his Microsoft stock each month to diversify his holdings. One might think he knows exactly the best time to sell or hold shares in his own company. However, Gates recognizes that stocks are different than companies, and even he can't predict the market's reaction to the events that impact Microsoft. His choice to sell "small" amounts of stock over time is a strategy intended to maximize his gains.

Bill Gates' plan illustrates the fact that dollar-cost averaging can be applied not only to index funds but to any significant investment holding. The bond ladder is an example of dollar cost averaging for fixed income investments. The reality is this: buying or selling is not usually an "all or nothing" decision. Often a graduated and staged move, in or out, is far more conservative and helps shield the average price paid or received from excessive volatility.

Dollar-cost averaging–perhaps even dollar-value averaging–is important to keep in mind when deciding how to manage risk when investing or when liquidating investment holdings. Having (and executing) a planned and gradual entry or exit approach ensures that you separate the strategic decision of asset allocation from the tactical, market-timing decision which is impossible to get right on a consistent basis. However, neither averaging strategy can guarantee a profit or protect against a loss of portfolio value.

For those who believe that successful investing requires more sophisticated concepts, we conclude this chapter with thoughts from David F. Swensen, money manager for the Yale University endowment fund, which stood at $16.7 billion in assets, with an 8.9% return for the year (and an impressive 8.9% return for the decade) ending June 30, 2010. The Yale Endowment Fund model has been copied by many universities across the country. Swensen offered this thought for individual investors seeking to manage their own portfolios: "Forget about making fancy market moves and focus on long-term gains . . . and, definitely ignore the advice of CNBC . . . whose investing strategies come with heavy commissions and costly tax consequences."

For instance, consider a diversified portfolio with allocations of 30% domestic stocks, 15% foreign stocks, and 5% emerging-market stocks, plus 20% in real estate index funds and 15% each in Treasury bonds and Treasury inflation-protected securities (TIPS).

"If the dollar declines dramatically, you have foreign and emerging-market equities," Swensen says. "When you are putting fresh money to work you put it in an asset class where you are underweight and take money out of a class that is overweight." Even though a declining dollar may fuel inflation, a diversified portfolio provides a hedge–an exact image of the portfolio rebalancing strategy discussed earlier in this book.

Swensen's final words of advice: Take yourself "off the hook" by not becoming anxious when markets decline. Stick strictly to the long view, he recommends, and "pursue the sensible long-term policy, look at it over a 5-to-10-year period. Don't look at five months."

Chapter 15
Building a Rip Van Winkle Portfolio:
A Radically Simple Approach
to Long-Term Wealth
(But first fire your stockbroker!)

> To invest successfully does not require a stratospheric IQ, unusual business insights, or inside information. What's needed is a sound intellectual framework for making decisions and the ability to keep emotions from corroding the framework.
> – Warren Buffett

For those savvy investors who recognize the wisdom of the Rip Van Winkle investment style, superior returns can be reached by simply purchasing two ETFs and calling it a day. Nevertheless, even better returns are achievable by diligently investing right. Returns can be further enhanced through proper portfolio allocation and maintenance, which includes annual rebalancing.

Merriam-Webster defines religion as "a cause, principle, or system of beliefs held to with ardor." *RVW Investing* is an empirical and highly scientific method of investing which has withstood the test of time. For those of us who have "seen the light" of long-term, index-based investing, Rip Van Winkle is elevated to the status of *prophet* . . . proclaiming a "strategic passivity pays" approach to investment success.

Much like a religious belief, RVW investing demands dedication–and unwavering commitment–to a set of core principles that have also withstood the test of time. In this chapter we will review the necessary fundamentals of RVW portfolio construction and describe a simple two-ETF equity portfolio suitable for small investors. Moreover, we will outline the reasons we believe nuance and sophistication can also be artfully applied to these fundamentals to further mitigate risk and enhance returns.

Fundamentalist Rip

To be clear, successful investing requires less action than most investors, large and small alike, are comfortable with. The Rip Van Winkle approach is based on Nobel Prize-winning theories which demonstrate how index investing consistently beats active management. It relies on more advanced research, which demonstrates that value stocks, small-cap stocks, and international stocks usually outperform the major market indexes. Proper portfolio diversification has repeatedly been shown in studies to reduce risk and is employed in this strategy.

1. *Invest in index funds or ETFs* Indexes tend to outperform active managers more than 80% of the time by eliminating individual stock risk and sector risk, leaving only pure market risk.

2. *Diversify across asset classes* Improper asset allocation is responsible for more than 90% of the volatility in a portfolio. The greater the diversity of your holdings, the smaller the risk associated with any one component of a portfolio.

3. *Ruthless cost-cutting* Reduce the layers of expenses (taxes and management fees) that impair returns.

These three fundamentals can be applied using an exceedingly simple formula. The basic portfolio below is not recommended for an investor whose total investment is greater than $100,000. For those who have more than $100,000 to invest but wish to avoid the headache and lost sleep that might result from employing the more complex strategies discussed later in this chapter, there are financial advisors who will provide these services for a modest fee. We do recommend, however, that you employ *only* those advisors who both have the expertise and platform to manage ETF portfolios for tax efficiency and also believe in, and apply, the RVW philosophy.

While the simplicity of **RVW Investing** is appealing to many, sophisticated investors should rely on a skilled investment advisor to develop an enhanced approach to asset allocation and the selection of intelligent indexing. The basic RVW equity allocation will beat 80% of managers, but our custom portfolios may include gold, oil, resources, and non-cap-weighted indexes, which will do even better than that.

You can put the RVW approach to work immediately and maintain the portfolio in less than one hour annually. Here's how:

Step 1   **Fire your non-RVW asset manager** and move the funds to an *RVW Investing* advisor or discount brokerage.

Step 2   **Create a simple asset allocation**, as outlined below, and work with your RVW advisor to determine a proper equity-bond ratio, bearing in mind that, for the larger investable amounts, the key question is: *For whom are the investments actually being made?* (If an allocation in bonds is not appropriate because you are very young or have less than $100,000 to invest, skip Step 3).

The general rule in applying the simple RVW Portfolio Asset Allocation Model®, the general rule is to subtract one's age from 120 and allocate that amount to the equity percentage. For example, a twenty-year-old should have 100% in equities and 0% in bonds; a seventy-year-old should have 50% in equities and bonds alike.

Step 3 **Determine whether you should be in taxable or tax-free bonds** considering both your marginal tax rate and relative interest rates of both categories. (A quick call to your tax adviser will reveal your combined marginal tax rate and your exposure to the Alternative Minimum Tax.)

Step 4 **Implement the portfolio** If you are investing any portion of the funds into equities for the first time, we suggest you stage that transfer over a period of three to nine months, in a staged and planned manner, to avoid timing the market. (Funds already in equities should immediately be moved into the *RVW Investing* equity portfolio.)

Step 5 **Redo this calculation annually** to rebalance the portfolio and check the taxable vs. tax-free bond allocation.

For smaller investors, those with less than $100,000, the first step of the simple formula is to allocate 75% of their assets into an ETF representing the broad stock market, such as the Vanguard Total Stock Market ETF (symbol: VTI). This ETF includes small-cap stocks, which research shows are likely to outperform the more popularly followed indexes such as the S&P 500®. Their remaining 25% should be allocated in an international fund, such as the Vanguard FTSE All-World ETF (symbol: VEU), which includes international stocks of both established and emerging foreign markets. Once again, taking volatility into account, research has shown that returns on international stocks beat the US markets over the long term. Through annual rebalancing, even smaller RVW investors are likely to generate better returns than more than 80% of mutual fund managers.

Asset Allocation

The basic portfolio above has a distinct disadvantage. While it does capture all of the key advantages of a well diversified global index-based approach, it lacks the nuance necessary to optimize profit potential. Moreover, by neglecting to include bonds, the portfolio will be more volatile than an optimum portfolio and will not generate sufficient cash distributions.

The first enhancement to **RVW Investing** is a little "elbow grease" applied to asset allocation, which will lead to more restful sleep and potentially greater wealth. While hard work is anathema to old Rip, statistics prove there is an appropriate time and place.

More than four decades ago, Nobel Prize-winning economists Franco Modigliani and Merton Miller demonstrated the intrinsic relationship between risk and reward. They demonstrated that asset classes with greater risk profiles generated higher average returns. Building on their research, Eugene Fama and Kenneth French proved a clear relationship exists between market capitalization, growth rates, and returns.

When it comes to investing in equities, according to **RVW Investing** principles, the only real decision most investors need to make is the portion of overall assets to place into stocks and how to allocate those assets between the different classes of stocks. Many studies have shown that more than 90% of investment returns are due to asset allocation and less than 10% of the returns are related to timing and stock selection. Since timing and selection are normally not possible, asset allocation is the only factor that can have an impact and should be the major focus of any investment strategy.

Investors, however, must not only determine their optimum mix of stock indexes, they must also decide how much to allocate to fixed-income securities. It is arguable that a one-size-fits-all portfolio of ETFs could be constructed, but, in reality, each investor has unique needs for cash flow and retirement planning and must, therefore, customize his own bond exposure and adjust that over time.

Risk control may be achieved through diversification. By risk, we mean volatility, and volatility is the degree to which returns vary from their average. The blending of various asset classes and styles reduces risk resulting in smoother (less volatile) returns and smoother returns result in better long-term growth of portfolios. The illustrations below demonstrate the power of smoother returns.

Compare these hypothetical annual returns for three different asset classes: p

	A	B	C
YEAR 1	45%	-12%	10%
YEAR 2	- 20%	35%	10%
TOTAL	25%	23%	20%

Which investment produces the best result by the end of the second year? As shown below, while the sum of the annual returns of Asset A is higher than B or C, the value of the investment at the end of the second year is lower. This is because the volatility of Asset A is greater than that of B or C. Asset C, which has no volatility, actually produces the highest asset value by the end of the second year.

	A	GROWTH OF $100	B	GROWTH OF $100	C	GROWTH OF $100
YEAR 1	45%	$145	-12%	$88	10%	$110
YEAR 2	- 20%	$116	35%	$119	10%	$121

As this hypothetical example illustrates, the smoother the returns, the better the end result. Assets A, B, and C are assumed to be negatively correlated. This means the annual returns each behave differently in any given year. Observe the result of combining these asset classes:

	A	B	C	COMBINED GROWTH	GROWTH OF $100
YEAR 1	45%	-12%	10%	14.3%	$114
YEAR 2	- 20%	35%	10%	8.3%	$124

This final illustration demonstrates the benefit of *risk control through diversification*. And it also reveals the greater importance of diversifying among asset classes and styles that are negatively correlated when constructing a portfolio.

Rebalancing

While benign neglect is an important component of the RVW approach, it is not the most efficient way to maintain a portfolio with a more complex asset allocation. We believe you should completely ignore market moves and not worry about day-to-day variations in your portfolio value. Nevertheless, some "preventive maintenance" is needed to maintain a portfolio's equilibrium.

Over time, asset classes perform differently and your portfolio composition will drift away from the targeted allocations–it will become *unbalanced*. It is important to sell some of the leaders and use the proceeds to buy more of the laggards, rebalancing to bring expected performance back to the original plan. Philosophically, this step assures that the investor–and not the market–determines and maintains the asset allocation within the portfolio.

Examining data from Morningstar, Inc., author Richard A. Ferri has determined that investors who use this form of "strategic" asset-allocation investing earn superior results compared to either those who attempt to time the markets ("tactical investors") or those strategists who merely buy and hold their investments. According to Ferri's analysis, the investor who annually rebalanced his portfolio from 2000 to 2009 achieved a 3.3% advantage compared to the 2.4% of the buy-and-hold strategists, and more than doubled the paltry 1.4% benefit obtained by the market-timing tactitians.

In *The Index Investing Book,* Ferri attributes this to the fact that financial markets don't perform better or worse simply because one person is buying and another is selling. When one investor buys at the "right" time it simply means another sold at the wrong time:

> Investors who lose with their tactical asset allocation strategies indirectly provide excess returns to investors who religiously rebalance their strategic allocation. This occurs because rebalancing naturally forces investors to sell some amount of their better-performing investments and buy more of their worse-performing ones. Although it seems counterintuitive to do this, over time, ***rebalancing increases portfolio returns and lowers risk.*** (emphasis added)

Strategic asset allocation and rebalancing represents a real wealth transfer that takes place in the marketplace. This return is enough to make up all the fund fees and trading costs that index fund investors incur, leaving these investors with very-close-to-market returns. You can't do much better than that. As Ferri put it, "Any extra gain in one person's account means a loss in someone else's."

By having a well-defined asset allocation policy in place, and regularly rebalancing to maintain a steady allocation, you will automatically take profits by selling when the market is euphoric and prices are high, and buy when the market is depressed and prices are low. This takes advantage of the fact that at the times of greatest optimism, future returns are likely to be lower; and when things look worst, when there is blood in the streets, future returns are likely to be the highest.

Some Suggested Portfolios

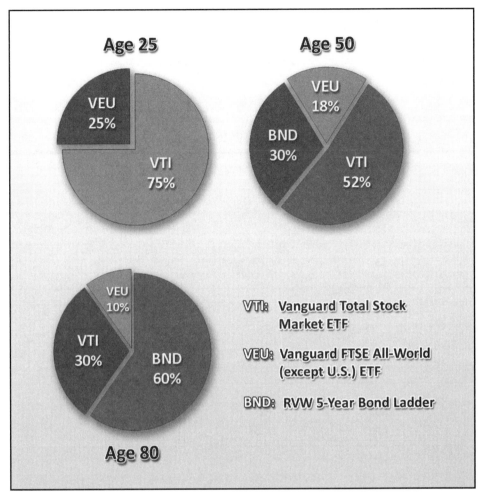

Source: RVW Research

Figure 15-1: These simple models show asset allocation varying according to an investor's age. Individual circumstances will vary in all cases. Regardless of age, it is the length of time one's money remains invested that has the greatest implication for any investor.

As an example of these concepts, some suggested portfolios are shown in Figure 15-1. Since personal circumstances vary dramatically, these would rarely be the exact portfolios. As mentioned previously, the percentage of bond allocation is usually approximated by using a basic formula of 120 minus the investor's age.

The results from these simple approaches are market-beating, as shown in Figure 15-2. In all cases, the RVW Portfolio outperformed the S&P 500®. For older investors, risk was reduced.

The results we show were obtained by substituting the PIMCO Total

Return Fund A, a bond mutual fund (symbol: PTTAX). Several Vanguard funds could be also be used. And larger investors are better served with a bond ladder, as described in Chapter 12, which accounts for specific income and tax considerations.

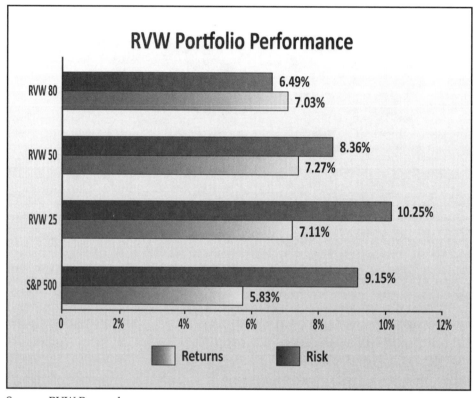

Source: RVW Research

Figure 15-2: These results show that the simplest RVW approaches outperform the market and adding a bond allocation to the portfolio reduces risks. These results are for the ten-year period ending in 2007. Larger investors would take similar approaches, using more ETFs to gain exposure to more asset classes and other investments to increase possible returns. In the end, these Rip Van Winkle portfolios will provide peace of mind, lower volatility than the markets, and superior returns.

New Age Rip–Indexing for Insomniacs

After reading this book, a person would have to be in complete denial to believe that he will earn greater long-term returns by attempting to time the market or selecting winning stocks. Nevertheless, many people are addicted to the market. They can't help but spend countless hours glued to CNBC or watching every tick on their computer screens. For such individuals, the temptation to buy and sell will be enormous. Moreover, they will have a hard time accepting market returns when they believe that they can do better by applying their own intelligence.

These market addicts are not lost for all time, destined to spend eternity with sub-market returns. They, too, can benefit from the power of Rip Van Winkle. Even market addicts cannot deny the fact that a core portfolio of ETFs is a wise foundation for success. Still, they seek to quench their thirst for instant profits by playing market moves. This is accomplished by trading "around" their core portfolio, making small directional bets that complement their index portfolio on an opportunistic basis.

> Guide your wealth ship by the stars, not the prevailing winds.
> – Rip Van Winkle Wisdom

One example of this approach using options is "writing" (or selling) calls against portfolio positions. A call is an option contract in which the buyer purchases the right to buy a security at a certain price at some time in the future "the exercise (or expiration) date." The seller, in turn, agrees to sell the security at that price, if and when the option is exercised. When the seller already owns the underlying security the option is called a *covered call*.

New Age RVW investors will sell these calls against portfolio positions. So long as these positions do not rise too quickly, the option expires and the seller pockets the premium (a fee paid by the buyer for the privilege of buying, whether they buy or not). If the position rises above the "strike" price, the option will be exercised and the investor will be forced to sell. In essence, this strategy will work to enhance returns in markets with limited upside volatility. For the investor with insomnia, it becomes the perfect elixir to allow him the opportunity to actively participate in the market and enhance his returns without undermining his newfound faith.

> I am essentially a Rip Van Winkle investor.
> – Warren Buffett

Long-time index investors and new converts alike have reason to be optimistic about their financial futures. With a defined strategy and a disciplined implementation plan, you will avoid the costly mistakes most others in the markets repeatedly make. A plan will avoid the overconfidence that can drive irrational buy and sell decisions. Bernstein recommends that you should "dare to be dull." Excitement is best found in other areas of your life. Buying and holding low-cost, market-beating index funds *should* be boring.

Why Your RVW Equity Portfolio Is Likely the Best Inflation Hedge

One of the biggest threats facing investors is the possibility that massive US budget deficits and the Federal Reserve's easy monetary policy will lead to significant inflation over the next five years or so.

For investors, over thirty-year periods, the return on stocks after inflation is virtually unaffected by the inflation rate. Although economists can show that average annual inflation in American history has been about 4%, the reality is that nearly all the inflation that the US has experienced in these past 235 years has occurred since the end of World War II. The prices of goods and services, as measured by the Consumer Price Index (which, conveniently, omits the cost of two basic necessities: food and energy), has risen tenfold since January 1947. Meanwhile, the S&P 500® Index, valued at 15.66 in January 1947, stood at 1328 in early April 2011–about 90 times higher.

> The stock market has predicted nine out of the past five recessions.
> – Paul Samuelson, Economist

The real return on stocks, in fact, during the inflationary postwar period is almost exactly the same as the returns in the nineteenth and early-twentieth centuries, when inflation was virtually nonexistent. And if you want income from your investments, consider this: stock dividends have risen faster than inflation both when prices are rising rapidly *and* when they are rising slowly. The *RVW Equity Portfolio* provides an overweighting to dividend-paying stocks and includes an allocation to gold. Gold typically does well in periods of high inflation.

Inflation will typically cause the dollar to decline in value and foreign stocks will act as an automatic hedge as foreign businesses and foreign earnings are translated into more dollars. International investing is therefore advisable (the **RVW Equity Portfolio** has approximately 25% invested in foreign-based companies). Inflation also impacts larger, US-based global companies, in which savvy investors are overweighted, because they have significant business activities located abroad. Both the value of those foreign assets and their earnings increase in relation to a falling dollar.

How do bonds fare? Bonds are promises to pay in dollars, and those dollars are fixed unless you hold Treasury inflation-protected securities ("TIPS") or other inflation-adjusted bonds. Currently, ten-year TIPS provide a real yield of less than 1% per year, and, recently, the yield on TIPS with maturities of less than five years has been negative. Ultimately, both the principal sum and the interest payments are devastated in terms of real value by inflation.

All investors must face the question of how much of their portfolio to allocate toward bonds. Applying the **Basic RVW Portfolio Asset Allocation Model**®, the general rule is to subtract one's age from 120 and allocate that number to the percentage of equities. For example, a twenty-year-old should have 100% invested in equities and 0% in bonds, but a seventy-year-old should have only 50% of their portfolio allocated to equities and the remaining 50% to bonds.

Under the **Complex RVW Portfolio Asset Allocation Model**®, you must first answer the question, "For whom are you actually investing?" Sometimes it's not for yourself but for your heirs. For those with significant wealth, the more complex RVW model requires engaging, at a minimum, in the following analysis:

- Determine how much cash will be needed from the portfolio for the lifestyle maintenance of the investor.

- Multiply by 33 to get the principal sum required to be set aside to provide the annual income needed, and that amount should be invested as described in the simple model above.

- RVW research shows that a 3% annual draw rate from a typical RVW portfolio will provide a virtually certain indefinite flow of income without draining the principal. The balance is invested according to the formula above, but based on the age of the person who will ultimately inherit the funds.

As an example, a single man age seventy-five with $20 million of available liquid assets and an annual income need of $50,000, whose sole heir is his twenty-year-old grandson, should invest as follows:

- 33 x $50,000 = $1,650,000 invested 45% in equities and 55% in bonds (120 − 75 = 45).

- The balance of $18,350,000 invested 100% in equities (120 − 20 = 100).

Before making any final asset allocation, however, an investor must consider all relevant factors such as other passive income sources, available liquidity, and the annual cash needs of the investor. At RVW, we employ a far more complex and integrated algorhythm to assist us in this process. Your self-discipline will be your greatest asset in investing. With a Rip Van Winkle portfolio, you will follow a plan that lets you keep your head while everyone else is losing theirs. Armed with the truth about the fees, inefficiencies, and fallacies that destine typical investors to sub-market returns, you have the power to take control of your financial future. You are now empowered to liberate yourself from the tyranny of brokers with "great" ideas and managers who churn your account for their own benefit.

If your investment advisor attempts to sell you the hottest new mutual fund or persuade you that he can divine the market's next move, you now know how to answer him: *"Gambling is for Las Vegas, I'm betting on Rip Van Winkle."*

What Makes RVW Investing *Different?*

1. We utilize no proprietary products, hedge funds, or bond funds. Our clients invest directly in the financial instruments they choose to own, obtaining favorable institutional pricing.

2. We are strategic advisors rather than tacticians. We make slow, measured moves, never attempting market-timing or picking stocks. We are CPAs and Registered Investment Advisers with fiduciary responsibilities, not stockbrokers.

3. Our clients have their own accounts at Schwab Institutional. In addition to the distinct advantage of institutional pricing, they enjoy realtime online access to their account information.

4. Unlike brokers, we have a fiduciary responsibility to our clients. We do not receive commissions, kickbacks, or other selling incentives. We work solely on behalf of our clients.

Afterword

> Our investigation found a financial snake pit rife with greed, conflicts of interest, and wrongdoing.
>
> — *Wall St. and the Financial Crisis*
> US Senate Report, April 2011

Wall Street would have you, the average investor, believe that you must subscribe to its "Conventional Wisdom." The product of decades of carefully planned and orchestrated marketing, Conventional Wisdom contends that investing is a specialized science requiring unique analytical skills and training. If you try to steer your own investment course, you are destined to become the proverbial "bull in the china shop"–and you can be sure things will turn out badly.

According to Conventional Wisdom, therefore, you should turn your investments over to a professional stockbroker or "financial advisor," who, like a trusted family member, will place your interests above his own and those of his brokerage firm. This financial advisor has sophisticated tools that allow him to pick undervalued stocks or time the market. His firm has an team of analysts who, likewise, can pick out undervalued stocks or tell you when to get in or out of the market. Relying on these professionals is the only way to succeed.

THE TRUTH ABOUT INVESTING IS <u>VERY</u> DIFFERENT! HERE ARE EIGHT THINGS YOUR BROKER WON'T TELL YOU

1. Neither Your Broker Nor His Firm's Analysts Can Successfully Pick Undervalued Stocks

In 2002, a five-year-old girl who chose stocks randomly from pieces of paper outperformed a top financial analyst by more than 50%. That same year, the cumulative returns on all stocks rated either "sell" or "hold" by Wall Street analysts outperformed all of the stocks rated "buy." That same year, 80% of all managed stock mutual funds underperformed the S&P 500® Index. These are the secrets you aren't supposed to know: First, that any short-term price movements in the stock market are based on random forces that are impossible to predict, and second, that in order to add value to your investment portfolio, the active manager has to make the market average return, plus his cost. Year in and year out, fewer than 20% of active managers meet this benchmark. And over ten years, the number dwindles to about 5%.

2. Your Broker Is Not Good at Evaluating or Reporting Your Risk

Ask any ten brokers to explain the risk inherent in a given portfolio, and nine of them wouldn't know how to measure or explain the risk. Not only are brokerage firms not good at asking the right questions to gauge an individual's tolerance for risk, they choose not to adequately disclose risk on monthly statements.

3. You Would Be Better Off Not Trying to Time the Market

Research has proven that the best approach to investing is the long-term one. The so-called experts are no better at picking overall market trends than they are individual stocks. If you trade in and out of the market, you'll be saddled with brokerage expenses that chip away at your returns, and you'll potentially miss out on gains that long-term investors enjoy with much less effort.

4. You Are Paying Too Much in Commissions and Mutual Fund Expenses

Your typical broker wants you to trade stocks and bonds, not hold them—that's how he gets paid. The problem is, this active management style generates fees, which are your direct expenses that eat away at your investment returns. The same is true of mutual funds, which charge high fees in the form of sales loads and internal expense ratios–1.5% of funds managed, on average.

5. Your Broker Does Not Act in Your Best Interest

Unlike the broker in the television commercial who attends your son's soccer games and toasts your daughter's wedding, real brokers have fought hard to preserve their status as salesmen rather than professional advisors. In 2005, the brokerage lobbyists pushed for and eventually won the right to act in their own best interests instead of yours. The good news is, in most cases, you can eliminate the need for a broker, and for those situations in which professional advice is necessary, you can find conflict-free advice. See points 7 and 8 below.

6. Your Broker Always Has Conflicts of Interest

All major brokerage firms have been caught recommending their clients buy stocks specifically because the issuing companies brought banking income to the firms. Privately, the analysts knew the stocks were "dogs" or were "going to zero," but publicly they prodded you and me to *buy, buy, buy!* These types of conflicts still exist in the forms of proprietary products, such as mutual funds and variable annuities, that offer little in the way of added value but certainly add plenty to the brokerage firm's bottom line.

7. You Can Implement a Sound, Basic Investment Plan Yourself at Low Cost

In about ninety minutes, you can probably determine the kind of basic portfolio that is right for you. You can purchase the basic components of an index-based portfolio through one of three well-respected no-load mutual fund companies. You could also assemble a basic portfolio using low-cost Exchange-Traded Funds (ETFs) purchased through one of the discount online brokerages, but their representatives are not permitted to offer any specific advice. For more specific information about the benefits of enhanced indexing and optimum asset allocation, visit us on the Internet at *www.rvwinvesting.com.*

8. If You Need Professional Help, There Are Low-Cost, Conflict-Free Advisors Available

There are times when professional advice is essential. Fortunately, there are conflict-free advisors who will pledge to put your interests first. You can find one in your area at *www.napfa.org,* or visit our website for more information.

Don't Count on Your Index Mutual Fund to Beat Its Benchmark Index

Actively managed stock funds fail to match their benchmark indexes more often than most mutual fund investors might imagine. They seek out funds with low expenses, low or no sales loads, and expect to match the performance of the fund's namesake.

Sadly, fund managers churn their portfolios, making wrong decisions when it comes to choosing what to buy and what to hold, realizing capital gains that pass to investors, and racking up other expenses paid for with fund revenue–all to the detriment of the shareholders.

As proof of this, the Standard & Poor's organization tracks actively managed funds by asset class and measures their performance against their benchmarks by creating equal-weighted portfolios to match the index. This is the same basic portfolio strategy discussed in Chapter 8.

By most measures, 2010 was another winning year for the US stock markets. But . . . take a look at the statistics for the year ended December 31, 2010 and decide whether you would have preferred the actively managed funds your broker is recommending or the equal-weighted approach that is a prominent component of *RVW Investing*.

And as you peruse these next few charts, consider what columnist Brett Arends counsels in his article in *The Wall Street Journal*, "Five things you should know about funds" (April 3, 2011):

1. *What are the fund's total fees, and where do they go?*

 How much does all this matter? Fund companies typically do better than you do, just as Las Vegas casinos typically make out better than Las Vegas tourists. Over 30 years, a fund earning 7% a year, with no fees, would turn $10,000 into $81,500. A fund charging a 5.75% sales load, with expenses of 1.5%: just $49,500. That's barely half the profits.

2. *Does the fund manager eat his own cooking?*

 Most fnd managers have no money in their own funds. No kidding. Warren Buffett is one of the richest men in the world, but he holds 99% of his wealth in his own investment vehicle, Berkshire Hathaway, alongside his investors. It shows.

3. *Will the fund company put your interests before its own?*

 The bigger the fund gets, the less likely it is to keep outperforming. Elephants don't dance. As new money pours into a successful mutual fund, even the best managers find it harder and harder to make great investments. Investors do less well. The fund company takes in a management fee on greater and greater assets. By definition, this problem generally afflicts only successful mutual funds anyway. If a fund company puts investors first, it will shut a mutual fund to new money fast, when the fund is still pretty small. Some do. Plenty of others don't.

4. Do your fund's performance figures mean anything?

Your broker will probably try to sell you funds that have done well over a one, three, or five-year period. It may mean something. But it may not mean anything at all. Why? First, the fund may have changed managers. Great investment is an art, not merely science. If it could be transferred from person to person, everyone would outperform. Second, good performance over a few years is probably pure luck. Do the math. There are thousands of mutual funds on the market. Over any given time period, some of them must do well. Brokers and fund companies market the ones that have done well, while quietly ignoring the others under the carpet. It doesn't mean all fund performance figures are worthless. A fund manager who has done well over a decade or more probably has what it takes. But all performance figures need to be taken with skepticism.

5. Who runs the fund–management or marketing?

Traditional investment managers tried to manage risk. They tried to buy attractive securities at attractive prices. If they couldn't find any they liked, they held cash and waited for better opportunities. Do you think that's still how it works? Not at most big mutual fund companies. Instead, they stick each manager in a "style box"–large-cap growth, small-cap value, and so on. The manager must buy only stocks within that box–maybe with a little leeway. A mid-cap growth manager must buy mid-cap growth stocks, even if they're overvalued. He can't touch small- or large-cap stocks, even if they're cheap. He has to stick close to "benchmarks." He can't hold cash. He has to be fully invested at all times. All sorts of bad things can follow.

Arends summarized the situation by writing:

> Mutual-fund companies will tell you they don't want
> to "time the market." OK. But it's notable that the marketing
> departments love this system. It makes funds easy to sell,
> outsources risk management to the client and covers their rear.
> If the market goes up, the funds aren't left behind. If the market
> tanks? "Oh, that's the market. Everyone's down." Sure. That's
> because "everyone" used the same system.

One final thought in this regard should help to keep everything in its
proper perspective. Market-timing depends entirely on the fully functional
crystal ball that none of us has. So, for those who think they can accurately
and consistently forecast market movements, imagine that you met a tarot
card reader on January 1, 2011. He predicted the natural disaster and
nuclear accident in Japan, the world's third-largest economy. He predicted
political and social turmoil across the Arab world, the war between NATO
and Libya, and the spike in oil prices. He even anticipated that Standard &
Poor's would downgrade its outlook on US government debt from "stable"
to "negative" and intuited that Europe's national debt problems would
worsen.

Knowing all that, could you have possibly predicted how US and
international stocks would behave in the ensuing period?

Source: RVW Investing / Standard & Poor's

Percentage of Actively Managed Equity Mutual Funds Failing to Match Their Benchmark Index's Performance

FUND CATEGORY	BENCHMARK INDEX	1-YEAR (%)	3-YEARS (%)	5-YEARS (%)
ALL DOMESTIC EQUITY FUNDS	S&P COMPOSITE 1500	49.31	51.68	57.63
ALL LARGE-CAP FUNDS	S&P 500	65.72	57.65	61.83
ALL MID-CAP FUNDS	S&P MIDCAP 400	73.75	83.90	78.19
ALL SMALL-CAP FUNDS	S&P SMALLCAP 600	53.42	70.11	63.02
ALL MULTI-CAP FUNDS	S&P COMPOSITE 1500	63.90	60.84	66.28
LARGE-CAP GROWTH FUNDS	S&P 500 GROWTH	49.86	78.67	82.00
LARGE-CAP CORE FUNDS	S&P 500	76.25	60.83	63.20
LARGE-CAP VALUE FUNDS	S&P 500 VALUE	71.30	31.44	34.67
MID-CAP GROWTH FUNDS	S&P MIDCAP 400 GROWTH	83.65	94.89	82.14
MID-CAP CORE FUNDS	S&P MIDCAP 400	87.18	83.64	82.00
MID-CAP VALUE FUNDS	S&P MIDCAP 400 VALUE	57.73	71.72	71.76
SMALL-CAP GROWTH FUNDS	S&P SMALLCAP 600 GROWTH	61.63	83.59	72.68
SMALL-CAP CORE FUNDS	S&P SMALLCAP 600	59.27	65.78	60.21
SMALL-CAP VALUE FUNDS	S&P SMALLCAP 600 VALUE	39.52	52.94	51.81
MULTI-CAP GROWTH FUNDS	S&P COMPOSITE 1500 GROWTH	47.37	85.28	78.79
MULTI-CAP CORE FUNDS	S&P COMPOSITE 1500	70.67	56.16	61.22
MULTI-CAP VALUE FUNDS	S&P COMPOSITE 1500 VALUE	68.63	50.96	59.35
REAL ESTATE FUNDS	S&P BMI US REIT	75.71	72.57	68.83

Source: Standard & Poor's, CRSP. For periods ending December 31, 2010.
Outperformance is based upon equal-weight fund counts.

Average U.S. Equity Fund Performance (Equal Weighted) vs S&P Benchmarks

FUND CATEGORY	1-YEAR (%)	3-YEARS (%)	5-YEARS (%)
S&P COMPOSITE 1500	16.38	-2.15	-2.65
ALL DOMESTIC EQUITY FUNDS	18.61	-1.06	3.06
S&P 500	15.05	-2.86	2.29
ALL LARGE CAP FUNDS	13.84	-2.77	2.16
S&P MIDCAP 400	26.64	3.53	5.74
ALL MID CAP FUNDS	24.14	0.77	4.57
S&P SMALLCAP 600	26.32	3.02	4.65
ALL SMALL CAP FUNDS	26.16	1.69	4.12
S&P COMPOSITE 1500	16.38	-2.15	-2.65
ALL MULTI CAP FUNDS	63.90	60.84	66.28
S&P 500 GROWTH	15.04	-0.49	3.60
LARGE CAP GROWTH FUNDS	14.95	-2.47	2.41
S&P 500	15.05	-2.86	2.29
LARGE CAP CORE FUNDS	13.06	-2.97	1.89
S&P 500 VALUE	15.10	-5.36	0.87
LARGE CAP VALUE FUNDS	13.54	-3.00	2.11
S&P MIDCAP 400 GROWTH	30.55	4.74	6.66
MID CAP GROWTH FUNDS	26.10	0.04	4.90
S&P MIDCAP 400	26.64	3.53	5.74
MID CAP CORE FUNDS	23.16	0.96	3.81
S&P MIDCAP 400 VALUE	22.78	2.27	4.71
MID CAP VALUE FUNDS	21.52	1.70	4.41
S&P SMALLCAP 600 GROWTH	28.01	3.27	5.16
SMALL CAP GROWTH FUNDS	27.10	0.25	4.00
S&P SMALLCAP 600	26.32	3.02	4.65
SMALL CAP CORE FUNDS	25.45	1.98	3.99
S&P SMALLCAP 600 VALUE	24.72	2.61	4.06
SMALL CAP VALUE FUNDS	25.85	3.55	4.48
S&P COMPOSITE 1500 GROWTH	16.71	0.06	3.92
MULTI CAP GROWTH FUNDS	18.03	-2.08	2.99
S&P COMPOSITE 1500	16.38	-2.15	2.65
MULTI CAP CORE FUNDS	15.63	-1.856	2.55
S&P COMPOSITE 1500 VALUE	16.06	-4.46	1.30
MULTI CAP VALUE FUNDS	15.41	-2.97	1.45
S&P BMI U.S. REIT	28.46	0.62	2.91
REAL ESTATE FUNDS	23.96	-1.13	2.01

Source: Standard & Poor's, CRSP. For periods ending December 31, 2010. Outperformance is based upon equal weight fund counts. Index returns do not include payment of any sales charges or od fees an investor would pay to purchase the securities they represent. Such costs would lower performance. Past performance is not an indication of future results.

Percentage of Actively Managed Bond Mutual Funds Failing to Match Their Benchmark Index's Performance

FUND CATEGORY	BENCHMARK INDEX	1-YEAR (%)	3-YEARS (%)	5-YEARS (%)
GOVERNMENT LONG FUNDS	BARCLAYS LONG GOVERNMENT	94.12	65.96	68.18
GOVERNMENT INTERMEDIATE FUNDS	BARCLAYS INTERMEDIATE GOVERNMENT	68.29	58.70	68.09
GOVERNMENT SHORT FUNDS	BARCLAYS 1-3 YEAR GOVERNMENT	58.62	58.70	75.00
INVESTMENT GRADE LONG FUNDS	BARCLAYS LONG GOVERNMENT/CREDIT	76.15	72.73	69.79
INVESTMENT GRADE INTERMEDIATE FUNDS	BARCLAYS INTERMEDIATE GOVERNMENT/CREDIT	30.00	44.59	55.75
HIGH-YIELD FUNDS	BARCLAYS HIGH YIELD	75.50	92.09	92.37
MORTGAGE-BACKED SECURITIES FUNDS	BARCLAYS MORTGAGE-BACKED SECURITIES	21.67	72.00	83.67
GLOBAL INCOME FUNDS	BARCLAYS GLOBAL AGGREGATE	38.53	55.56	64.58
EMERGING MARKETS DEBT FUNDS	BARCLAYS EMERGING MARKETS	34.48	40.00	43.75
GENERAL MUNICIPAL DEBT FUNDS	S&P NATIONAL AMT-FREE MUNICIPAL BOND	60.67	77.65	86.08
CALIFORNIA MUNICIPAL DEBT FUNDS	S&P CALIFORNIA AMT-FREE MUNICIPAL BOND	84.21	90.48	97.50
NEW YORK MUNICIPAL DEBT FUNDS	S&P NEW YORK AMT-FREE MUNICIPAL BOND	64.71	91.67	94.29

Source: Standard & Poor's, CRSP. For periods ending December 31, 2010.
Outperformance is based upon equal-weight fund counts.

Average Fixed Income Fund Performance (Equal Weighted) vs Their Benchmarks

FUND CATEGORY	1-YEAR (%)	3-YEARS (%)	5-YEARS (%)
BARCLAYS LONG GOVERNMENT	9.44	5.64	5.70
GOVERNMENT LONG FUNDS	6.16	5.23	5.32
BARCLAYS INTERMEDIATE GOVERNMENT	4.97	4.93	5.40
GOVERNMENT INTERMEDIATE FUNDS	4.55	4.79	5.00
BARCLAYS 1-3 YEAR GOVERNMENT	2.38	3.46	4.32
GOVERNMENT SHORT FUNDS	2.64	3.33	3.97
BARCLAYS LONG GOVERNMENT/CREDIT	10.16	6.78	5.92
INVESTMENT-GRADE LONG FUNDS	8.76	5.86	5.53
BARCLAYS INTERMEDIATE GOVERNMENT/CREDIT	5.89	5.40	5.53
INVESTMENT-GRADE INTERMEDIATE FUNDS	7.04	5.35	5.13
BARCLAYS 1-3 YEAR GOVERNMENT/CREDIT	4.15	5.24	5.27
INVESTMENT-GRADE SHORT FUNDS	4.22	3.05	3.59
BARCLAYS HIGH YIELD	15.12	10.38	8.92
HIGH YIELD FUNDS	13.91	7.61	7.05
BARCLAYS MORTGAGE BACKED SECURITIES	5.36	6.52	6.33
MORTGAGE-BACKED SECURITIES FUNDS	6.61	5.14	5.11
BARCLAYS GLOBAL AGGREGATE	5.55	5.75	6.67
GLOBAL INCOME FUNDS	7.94	6.15	6.29
BARCLAYS EMERGING MARKETS	12.84	8.87	8.34
EMERGING MARKETS DEBT FUNDS	13.72	8.14	8.30
S&P NATIONAL AMT-FREE MUNICIPAL BOND	2.30	3.71	3.86
GENERAL MUNICIPAL DEBT FUNDS	1.99	2.90	3.01
S&P CALIFORNIA AMT-FREE MUNICIPAL BOND	3.29	3.49	3.73
CALIFORNIA MUNICIPAL DEBT FUNDS	2.16	2.42	2.63
S&P NEW YORK AMT-FREE MUNICIPAL BOND	2.26	4.00	4.04
NEW YORK MUNICIPAL DEBT FUNDS	1.96	3.18	3.25

Source: Standard & Poor's, CRSP. For periods ending December 31, 2010. Outperformance is based upon equal weight fund counts. Index returns do not include payment of any sales charges or od fees an investor would pay to purchase the securities they represent. Such costs would lower performance. Past performance is not an indication of future results.